WeightWatchers®
DiscoverPlan

PIZZA & *pasta*

First published in Great Britain by
Simon & Schuster UK Ltd, 2010.
A CBS Company

Copyright © 2010, Weight Watchers
International, Inc.

SIMON AND SCHUSTER
ILLUSTRATED BOOKS
Simon & Schuster UK
222 Gray's Inn Road
London WCIX 8HB
www.simonandschuster.co.uk

Weight Watchers and **POINTS** are the registered
trademarks of Weight Watchers International Inc.
Discover Plan™ and the **Discover Plan**™ logo are
trademarks of Weight Watchers International Inc.,
and all are used under its control by Weight Watchers
(UK) Ltd.

Weight Watchers Publications Team:
Jane Griffiths, Nina McKerlie and Fiona Smith
Simon and Schuster Project Editor: **Anna Hitchin**
Photography by **Steve Lee**
Styling by **Rachel Jukes**
Food preparation and styling by **Penny Stephens**
Design and typesetting by **Fiona Andreanelli**

Recipes by Carol Tennant: Creamy pepper pancetta pasta;
Prawn and tomato pasta bake; Pepperoni pizza; Bucatini
with meatballs; Balsamic chicken pizza; Balsamic roasted
red onion pizza with feta; Green vegetable pasta; Roasted
Mediterranean vegetable pizza; Mixed tomato pizza; Pesto
prawn pizza; Green vegetable pasta; Pasta with cullen skink
sauce; Courgette, pesto and lemon pasta; Quick classic
pizza; Crema Italiana; Espresso biscotti.

Printed and bound in Singapore

A CIP catalogue for this book is available from
the British Library

Pictured on the front cover: Balsamic chicken
pizza, page 25.
Pictured on the back cover, from top to bottom: Balsamic
roasted red onion pizza with feta, page 26; Roasted cod
and butternut squash linguine, page 8; Crema Italiana,
page 59.

POINTS® value logo: You'll find this easy to read
POINTS value logo on every recipe throughout
this book. The logo represents the number of **POINTS**
values per serving each recipe contains. Weight Watchers
POINTS Weight Loss System is a simple way to lose
weight. As part of the Weight Watchers **Discover Plan**™
you'll enjoy eating delicious, healthy, filling foods that
help to keep you feeling satisfied for longer and in
control of both your portion sizes and your hunger.

Filling Foods are highlighted in green – like this. Focus
on these foods where you can – they keep you feeling
satisfied for longer.

Ⓥ This symbol denotes a vegetarian recipe and assumes
that, where relevant, free range eggs, vegetarian cheese,
vegetarian virtually fat free fromage frais, vegetarian low
fat crème fraîche and vegetarian low fat yogurts are used.
Virtually fat free fromage frais, low fat crème fraîche and
low fat yogurts may contain traces of gelatine so they are
not always vegetarian. Please check the labels.

❄ This symbol denotes a dish that can be frozen.

Recipe notes
Egg size Medium, unless otherwise stated.
All fruits and vegetables Medium size unless
otherwise stated.
Raw eggs Only the freshest eggs should be used.
Pregnant women, the elderly and children should avoid
recipes with eggs which are not fully cooked or raw.
Low fat spread Where a recipe states to use a low fat
spread, a light spread with a fat content of no less than
38% should be used.
Stock Stock cubes should be used in the recipes, unless
otherwise stated. Prepare them according to the packet
instructions.
Recipe timings These are approximate and meant to be
guidelines. Please note that the preparation time includes
all the steps up to and following the main cooking time(s).

Contents

Introduction

Pizza and pasta appeal to all ages, tastes and budgets. They're quick, **satisfying** and low in *POINTS* values so we're sure you'll enjoy making them again and again.

Pizza & Pasta is the latest cookbook from Weight Watchers, developed to work alongside the **Discover Plan**™. There are 60 new and satisfying recipes, many of which contain **Filling Foods** that can help to S-T-R-E-T-C-H your *POINTS* values so you are able to eat more and make your daily allowance go further. **Filling Foods** can also help you to stay satisfied for longer.

We know that both pizza and pasta are popular choices with our members and their families but they can often be high in *POINTS* values, particularly dishes with creamy sauces. With this fantastic new cookbook, you'll find you can enjoy many of your favourite Italian meals and still lose weight.

All the recipes are simple to follow and easy on the pocket too. You'll find an appetising collection of recipes ranging from meals for one and two, family meals, vegetarian dishes and delicious desserts. There are classic recipes such as Pasta Arrabbiata, Hawaiian Pizza and Spinach and Mushroom Cannelloni as well as a few more innovative dishes such as Pasta in a Paper Bag, Grilled Teriyaki Salmon and Pasta and Pesto Prawn Pizza. There's also a quick and easy chapter where most recipes are ready in 20 minutes or less.

All the recipes in *Pizza & Pasta* are easy to make and use healthy ingredients that are full of flavour. We hope you enjoy *Pizza & Pasta*.

Ingredients and Methods

YEAST Yeast is a live raising agent that can be bought fresh or dried.

The fresh variety or baker's yeast is usually available from bakers or the baking departments in supermarkets. It needs to be refrigerated and used within a few days so you should always check the 'use by' date. It can also be frozen, which is handy. Fresh yeast needs food (sugar) and warmth (hand hot water or milk) to activate it before adding it to the dry ingredients.

Dried yeast is simply an inactive form with the moisture removed and is available as 'dried' or 'instant dried'. All the recipes in this book use an instant dried yeast which is also called 'fast action', 'quick', or 'easy blend'. Dried yeast needs to be activated but it has a longer shelf life and can be stored at an ambient temperature. Instant dried yeast can be added along with the dried ingredients and will begin fermenting on contact with the added liquid. Its other advantage is that it only requires one proving or rising.

FLOUR The flour used for making bread or pizza dough should always be strong flour, whether it is white, brown or wholemeal flour. The gluten in strong flour gives the dough its elasticity. Gluten also traps the carbon dioxide released by the yeast to help to create a smooth texture.

KNEADING Kneading dough strengthens the gluten in the flour which makes the dough more stretchy and enables it to rise more easily.

SHAPING (STRETCHING) Once the dough has a soft and elastic consistency, it needs to be shaped or stretched. Roll out the dough on a clean and lightly floured surface or stretch it with your hands. Wet hands will help if you want to stretch the dough to a large size – 25 cm (10 inches) or more. Always use a non stick baking tray or mist the tray with low fat cooking spray. Avoid using your fingertips as too much pressure will kill the yeast.

PROVING (RISING) Once the dough has been kneaded and shaped, it needs to prove or rise. Cover it with a clean cloth and leave it in a warm, draught free place until doubled in size. The length of time it takes to prove properly depends on the quantity of dough and how much yeast it contains. The recipe will tell you how long to leave it to rise.

KNOCKING BACK Knocking back is the second stage of kneading which is necessary in some recipes, usually where fresh or ordinary dried (as opposed to instant dried) yeast has been used or if you are creating a rich dough (see step 5 for Panettone on page 58) where the dough needs to be softer.

Kneading for a second time redistributes the gases and creates a more even dough. Once kneaded the dough is shaped and given a second, shorter rising. Any dough recipe could be knocked back and allowed a second rising but it is not necessary when using instant dried yeast.

PASTA Dried pasta comes in many shapes and sizes. You can replace the pasta in these recipes with pasta you may have in the cupboard but it's useful to remember a few important points when doing so.

A thin sauce or a sauce with lots of chunky bits in it (such as ragu) works best with a wide pasta such as papparadelle or a pasta with a larger surface area such as fusilli. A thick sauce (such as pesto) will cling to most types of pasta but it could overwhelm a thin pasta such as angel hair or one of the smaller shapes.

Wholewheat or brown pasta has the same *POINTS* values as white pasta. Fresh pasta is quicker to cook and readily available, but the total *POINTS* values of a recipe may change.

Meals for one and two

With these **tempting** recipes which include ideas for all kinds of meals, ranging from a simple supper to a lunch party, cooking for **one or two** has never been easier.

Individual cheesy aubergine pizzas

Serves 2 | 10 *POINTS* values per recipe | Takes 30 minutes to prepare, **15** minutes to cook | **246** calories per serving

low fat cooking spray
½ x 144 g pack pizza base mix
For the topping:
1 small aubergine, sliced thinly
2 teaspoons pesto
2 tomatoes, sliced
75 g (2¾ oz) light mozzarella, drained
    and sliced
salt and freshly ground black pepper
fresh basil leaves, to garnish

1 Preheat the oven to Gas Mark 7/220°C/fan oven 200°C. Spray a non stick baking tray with the cooking spray and set aside.
2 Make up the dough according to the packet instructions, kneading for 5 minutes before dividing it in two. Shape each piece of dough into a 15 cm (6 inch) circle and place on the baking tray. Set aside in a warm place to rise for 10 minutes.
3 Meanwhile, heat a griddle pan or frying pan until it is really hot. Spray the aubergine slices with the cooking spray and then cook over a high heat for 3–4 minutes, turning once, until softened. Drain on kitchen paper.
4 Spread the dough with the pesto and top with the aubergine, tomato and mozzarella slices. Season and bake for 10–15 minutes until the dough is golden and the cheese is bubbling. Serve garnished with some basil leaves.

Variation...Use two small courgettes instead of the aubergines. Griddle long slices, cut with a potato peeler, instead of lots of little rings. The POINTS values will remain the same.

Roasted cod and butternut squash linguine

Serves 1 | **4½ POINTS** values per recipe | **Takes 20** minutes to prepare, **35** minutes to cook | **611** calories per serving

½ small butternut squash, *peeled, de-seeded and cut into small dice*
1 small red onion, *cut into thin wedges*
1 rosemary *sprig*
1 thyme *sprig*
low fat cooking spray
200 g (7 oz) skinless cod fillet
40 g (1½ oz) dried linguine
2 tablespoons fat free dressing
salt and freshly ground black pepper

1 Preheat the oven to Gas Mark 7/220°C/fan oven 200°C. Place the squash, onion and herbs in a large roasting tin. Spray with the cooking spray and roast for 20 minutes, stirring occasionally.

2 Season the cod and sit it on top of the squash and onion. Roast for a further 15 minutes until the vegetables are lightly charred and the cod flakes with a fork. Once cooked, flake the fish into chunks.

3 Meanwhile, bring a large pan of water to the boil, add the pasta and cook for 10–12 minutes or according to the packet instructions. Drain well and rinse.

4 Mix the dressing into the pasta, then add the vegetables and the cod along with any caramelised bits from the tin. Mix together well and serve.

ⓥ *Variation*…Use two carrots, peeled and chopped, instead of the butternut squash. The POINTS values will remain the same.

Pepperonata rigatoni

Serves 2 | **8** *POINTS* values per recipe | **Takes 30** minutes | **326** calories per serving

Pepperonata is a traditional antipasto dish, made of ready cooked red and yellow or orange **peppers**. Stir this quick version into **pasta** and you have a delicious meal.

1 red pepper, *halved and de-seeded*
1 yellow *or* orange pepper, *halved and de-seeded*
125 g (4½ oz) dried rigatoni *or* penne
low fat cooking spray
1 red onion, *sliced thinly into rings*
1 garlic clove, *crushed*
1 tablespoon thyme *leaves*
salt and freshly ground black pepper
15 g (½ oz) Parmesan cheese, *freshly grated, to serve*

1 Preheat the grill to High. Lay the peppers skin side up on the grill pan. Grill for 10 minutes until the skin is black and blistered. Place in a bowl, cover with cling film and leave to cool.

2 Bring a large pan of water to the boil, add the pasta and cook for 10–12 minutes or according to the packet instructions. Drain, reserving 2 tablespoons of the cooking liquid, then rinse.

3 Spray a non stick frying pan with the cooking spray and heat. Add the onion and cook over a low heat for 10 minutes until softened and beginning to caramelise.

4 Meanwhile, peel the skin from the peppers, slice thinly and add to the frying pan with the garlic and thyme. Season. Cook for a further 5 minutes. Add the reserved cooking liquid then toss into the pasta and sprinkle with the Parmesan cheese.

Herby chicken calzone

Serves 2 | **9½** *POINTS* values per recipe | **Takes 35** minutes to prepare, **15** minutes to cook | **307** calories per serving

low fat cooking spray
½ x 144 g pack pizza base mix
2 teaspoons dried mixed herbs
250 g (9 oz) skinless boneless chicken breast, *cut into strips*
1 courgette, *trimmed and grated*
4 cherry tomatoes, *halved*
10 fresh basil *leaves*
2 tablespoons sun-dried tomato purée
1 egg white, *lightly beaten, to glaze*

1 Preheat the oven to Gas Mark 7/220°C/fan oven 200°C. Spray a baking tray with the cooking spray and set aside.

2 Make up the dough according to the packet instructions, adding the mixed herbs before the water. Knead for 5 minutes, then return the dough to the mixing bowl, cover with a clean cloth and leave to prove while you prepare the filling.

3 Spray a non stick frying pan with the cooking spray, heat until sizzling and then add the chicken. Cook over a medium heat, stirring occasionally for 5 minutes until the chicken is golden and cooked through. Add the courgette and cook for 1 minute to allow some of the water to evaporate. Remove from the heat. Mix in the tomatoes and basil.

4 Divide the dough in two and knead each piece lightly. Shape into rounds approximately 18 cm (7 inches) in diameter and place on the baking tray. Spread the tomato purée over the bases and place the filling on one side of each circle. Brush the edges with a little water, fold over and pinch the edges together to seal. Leave in a warm place to prove for 5 minutes.

5 Brush with the egg white and bake for 15 minutes until golden. Serve either warm or cold.

Meals for one and two

Creamy pepper pancetta pasta

(5 POINTS VALUE)

Serves 1 | **5 POINTS** values per recipe | **Takes 10** minutes to prepare, **15** minutes to cook | **373** calories per serving

The lovely rich flavour of this sauce comes from cooking the **pepper** very slowly, which softens and caramelises it slightly, so don't rush it.

> 1 rasher smoked pancetta, chopped finely
> low fat cooking spray
> 1 shallot, chopped finely
> ½ red pepper, de-seeded and sliced finely
> 40 g (1½ oz) dried pasta shapes, such as conchiglie
> 50 g (1¾ oz) low fat soft cheese
> 2 or 3 tablespoons skimmed milk
> salt and freshly ground black pepper
> 2 teaspoons freshly grated Parmesan cheese, to serve

1 Heat a small non stick frying pan until hot and add the pancetta. Cook over a medium heat until browned and crispy. Remove from the pan, drain on kitchen paper and set aside.

2 Clean the excess fat from the pan and spray with the cooking spray. Add the shallot and red pepper. Cook over a low heat, about 12–15 minutes, adding a little water to the pan if the vegetables start to stick, until the pepper is very soft and just starting to brown.

3 Meanwhile, bring a large pan of water to the boil, add the pasta and cook for 7–9 minutes, or according to the packet instructions, until al dente. Drain well.

4 Return the pancetta to the pan along with the soft cheese and 2 tablespoons of the milk. Stir until the cheese has melted and is coating everything, adding the remaining tablespoon of milk if necessary. Season to taste.

5 Add the drained pasta and stir well. Serve sprinkled with the Parmesan cheese.

Spicy tomato tagliatelle

(3½ POINTS VALUE)

 Serves 1 | **3½ POINTS** values per recipe | **Takes 25** minutes | **210** calories per serving

This wonderfully simple and tasty dish brings out the fresh, sweet flavour of **cherry tomatoes**. Try to use both red and yellow cherry tomatoes, when yellow ones are in season.

> 40 g (1½ oz) dried tagliatelle
> low fat cooking spray
> 2 spring onions, chopped
> 140 g (5 oz) cherry tomatoes, preferably on the vine
> ½ red chilli, de-seeded and diced
> 1 tablespoon chopped fresh parsley
> salt and freshly ground black pepper
> 1 tablespoon freshly grated Parmesan cheese, to serve

1 Bring a large pan of water to the boil. Add the pasta and cook for 10–12 minutes or according to the packet instructions. Drain and rinse.

2 Spray a saucepan with the cooking spray and heat until sizzling. Add the spring onions and cook over a medium heat until just beginning to brown.

3 Add the tomatoes to the pan with the chilli. Cook over a low heat for 5 minutes, adding a little water if necessary, until they have softened but still retain some shape. Season and stir in the parsley.

4 Toss the tomato sauce into the pasta and serve sprinkled with the Parmesan cheese.

Tip…The sauce will be quite chunky, so if you prefer it smoother, simply cook it for 2–3 minutes longer and then mash or blend in a liquidiser.

Prawn and tomato pasta bake

Serves 2 | 12 *POINTS* values per recipe | Takes **30** minutes to prepare, **25** minutes to cook + cooling | **405** calories per serving

    low fat cooking spray
    1 small onion, chopped finely
    1 small red chilli, de-seeded and
       chopped finely
    1 garlic clove, chopped finely
    400 g can chopped tomatoes
    1 teaspoon dried oregano
    250 ml (9 fl oz) skimmed milk
    2 tablespoons sauce flour
    40 g (1½ oz) half fat Cheddar cheese,
       freshly grated
    75 g (2¾ oz) dried rigatoni
    100 g (3½ oz) cooked, peeled prawns
    75 g (2¾ oz) cherry tomatoes, halved
    1 tablespoon finely grated Parmesan cheese
    salt and freshly ground black pepper

1 Spray a medium saucepan with the cooking spray and place over a medium heat. Add the onion, reduce the heat and cook for about 5 minutes until softened.

Add a little water if the onion starts to stick. When the onion is soft, add the chilli and garlic and cook for 30 seconds or so. Add the tomatoes and oregano. Bring to the boil and simmer for 20–30 minutes until thickened. Season to taste and set aside.

2 Meanwhile, put the skimmed milk into another saucepan. Heat until warm but don't allow it to boil then remove from the heat and whisk in the sauce flour. Put the pan over a medium heat and bring slowly to a simmer, whisking often. Simmer for 2 minutes, whisking, then remove from the heat and add the Cheddar cheese. Stir until melted. Season and set aside.

3 Preheat the oven to Gas Mark 6/200°C/fan oven 180°C. Bring a large pan of water to the boil and add the pasta. Cook for 7 minutes then drain thoroughly.

4 Stir the prawns into the tomato sauce then add the pasta. Turn the mixture into a shallow 1.2 litre (2 pint) ovenproof dish. Pour over the cheese sauce then scatter over the cherry tomatoes, pressing them in slightly. Sprinkle with the Parmesan cheese.

5 Bake for 20–25 minutes. Remove from the oven and leave to stand for 10 minutes before serving.

Pepperoni pizza

6½ POINTS VALUE

❄ sauce only | **Serves 2** | **12½ POINTS** values per recipe |
Takes 25 minutes to prepare, **15** minutes to cook |
310 calories per serving

½ x 144 g pack pizza base mix
For the topping:
low fat cooking spray
½ small onion, chopped finely
1 garlic clove, crushed
a generous pinch of dried chilli flakes
1 teaspoon dried oregano
200 g can chopped tomatoes
1 yellow pepper, de-seeded and
    quartered lengthwise
30 g (1¼ oz) sliced pepperoni
50 g (1¾ oz) cherry tomatoes, halved
75 g (2¾ oz) light mozzarella, drained and sliced
25 g (1 oz) rocket leaves
salt and freshly ground black pepper

1 Spray a small saucepan with the cooking spray and place over a medium heat. Add the onion and garlic and cook for 5 minutes until softened, adding a little water, if necessary, to prevent sticking. Add the chilli flakes, oregano and chopped tomatoes. Bring to the boil and simmer for about 20 minutes until thickened.

2 Meanwhile, make up the pizza dough according to the packet instructions. Set aside in a bowl covered with a clean tea towel until needed.

3 Preheat the grill to High. Put the pepper quarters on to a baking tray, spray with the cooking spray and cook under the grill for about 5–7 minutes, turning once, until the skins have blackened. Remove from the grill, place in a bowl and leave to cool. When cool, peel off the skins and slice the peppers lengthwise into thick strips.

4 Preheat the oven to Gas Mark 7/220°C/fan oven 200°C. Divide the dough in half and shape each piece into a 20 cm (8 inch) circle. Spray a non stick baking tray with cooking spray and place the pizzas on it. Divide the tomato sauce between the bases then top with the pepperoni, pepper, tomatoes and mozzarella. Season.

5 Bake for 12–15 minutes until the dough is golden and the cheese is bubbling. Remove from the oven and transfer each pizza to a serving plate. Top each with half of the rocket and serve immediately.

Meals for one and two

Meat and Poultry

Chicken and broccoli conchiglie

Serves 1 | 4½ *POINTS* values per recipe | **Takes 20** minutes | **446** calories per serving

Conchiglie are ridged **pasta** shells. They're available in different sizes and sometimes they are multicoloured too.

> 40 g (1½ oz) dried conchiglie or pasta shells
> 110 g (4 oz) long stemmed broccoli or broccoli florets, trimmed
> low fat cooking spray
> 150 g (5½ oz) skinless boneless chicken breast, cut into strips
> 1 small red onion, sliced
> ½ red pepper, de-seeded and sliced
> 2 tablespoons light soy sauce
> 1 tablespoon sweet Thai chilli sauce
> salt and freshly ground black pepper
> 1 tablespoon fresh coriander leaves, to garnish

1 Bring a large pan of water to the boil, add the pasta and cook for 10–12 minutes or according to the packet instructions. Add the broccoli for the final 5 minutes of cooking time. Drain and rinse thoroughly.

2 Spray a non stick frying pan with the cooking spray and heat until hot. Add the chicken, onion and red pepper. Stir fry for 5 minutes until browned and cooked through.

3 Add the soy sauce and chilli sauce. Toss to coat. Stir in the pasta and broccoli and cook for 1 minute until everything is piping hot. Season and serve garnished with coriander leaves.

Tip…Long stemmed or purple sprouting broccoli have especially tender stems. They're available in the spring and summer.

Variation…For a veggie version, use 1 Quorn Fillet (50 g/1¾ oz), sliced, for 3 *POINTS* values per serving.

Here are plenty of **tasty ideas** for family meals as well as dishes for entertaining. Enjoy **fabulous recipes** such as Turkey Lasagne, Pasta Arrabbiata or Chorizo Pizza with Warm Potato Salad.

4 1/2 POINTS VALUE

Pasta arrabbiata

❄ sauce only | **Serves 4** | **18½ POINTS** values per recipe | **Takes 20** minutes | **357** calories per serving

250 g (9 oz) dried penne
low fat cooking spray
4 rashers lean back bacon, cut into
    thin strips
2 red onions, sliced
2 garlic cloves, crushed
1 red chilli, de-seeded and diced
2 x 400 g can chopped tomatoes
2 tablespoons tomato purée
2 tablespoons fresh basil leaves, torn,
    plus extra to garnish
salt and freshly ground black pepper

1 Bring a large pan of water to the boil, add the pasta and cook for 10–12 minutes or according to packet instructions. Drain and rinse thoroughly.
2 Meanwhile, spray a large, non stick pan with the cooking spray. Add the bacon, onions, garlic and chilli and cook, stirring over a medium heat for 5 minutes until the onions have softened. Add the chopped tomatoes and tomato purée and cook for 5 minutes until thickened slightly.
3 Add the basil and season. Add the drained pasta and stir to combine. Heat until piping hot then serve garnished with the extra basil leaves.

Variation...Extra lean back bacon would reduce the POINTS values to 3½ per serving.

Turkey lasagne

❄ **Serves 4** | 17 *POINTS* values per recipe | **Takes 25** minutes to prepare, **35** minutes to cook | **316** calories per serving

Quark is a very low fat soft cheese and works well in both sweet and savoury recipes.

low fat cooking spray
1 onion, chopped
1 courgette, sliced
250 g (9 oz) turkey steaks, cut into strips
400 g can chopped tomatoes with garlic
and herbs
140 g (5 oz) no pre cook lasagne
250 g tub Quark
50 g (1¾ oz) half fat Cheddar cheese,
freshly grated
10 cherry tomatoes
salt and freshly ground black pepper

1 Preheat the oven to Gas Mark 5/190°C/fan oven 170°C. Spray a large, lidded, non stick pan with the cooking spray. Add the onion and courgette and cook for 5 minutes until softened. Add the turkey strips and stir fry for 3 minutes until browned. Stir in the chopped tomatoes, bring to the boil, cover and cook for 10 minutes until the turkey is tender. Season.
2 Cover the bottom of a 1 litre (1¾ pint) dish with half of the turkey mixture. Lay four sheets of lasagne on top and repeat the layers, finishing with a layer of lasagne.
3 Mix the Quark with 4 tablespoons of water and half the Cheddar cheese. Spread the mixture over the top of the lasagne, making sure it is completely covered. Top with the remaining Cheddar cheese and the cherry tomatoes. Bake for 35 minutes until golden.

Variation...Instead of turkey steaks, you can use 250 g (9 oz) skinless chicken breasts. The POINTS values per serving will be 4½.

Sausage and rocket pasta salad

Serves 2 | 7 *POINTS* values per recipe | **Takes 20** minutes to prepare + **10** minutes cooling | **228** calories per serving

In this summery salad, the creamy mustard dressing complements the sausages beautifully and rocket adds just enough hot peppery flavour.

2 thick low fat pork sausages
75 g (2¾ oz) dried pasta bows
60 g (2 oz) asparagus tips
1 red pepper, de-seeded and diced
into 1 cm (½ inch) pieces
25 g (1 oz) rocket leaves
For the dressing:
4 tablespoons 0% fat Greek yogurt
2 teaspoons wholegrain mustard

1 Preheat the grill to medium and line the grill pan with foil. Cook the sausages for 7–8 minutes, turning until golden all over. Remove from the heat and when cool, slice each one into five pieces.
2 Meanwhile, bring a large pan of water to the boil, add the pasta and cook for 10–12 minutes, or according to the packet instructions, adding the asparagus tips for the final 5 minutes of cooking. Drain and rinse with cold water until cool. Drain again.
3 Mix together the dressing ingredients and toss with the sausage pieces, pasta, asparagus, red pepper and rocket.

Tip...Make this salad an hour in advance without the rocket, then cover and chill until required, mixing in the rocket before serving. This allows the flavours to develop.

Spicy turkey pizza

❄ topping only | **Serves 2** | **8 POINTS** values per recipe |
Takes 35 minutes | **335** calories per serving

Make the topping in advance and this pizza
is ideal for a last minute meal.

> low fat cooking spray
> 23 cm (9 inch) ready made thin and
>   crispy pizza base
> **For the topping:**
> 1 small onion, chopped finely
> 1 garlic clove, crushed
> 140 g (5 oz) turkey mince
> 2 teaspoons dried mixed herbs
> 210 g can chopped tomatoes
> 2 tomatoes, sliced
> 1 red chilli, de-seeded and diced
> salt and freshly ground black pepper

1 Preheat the oven to Gas Mark 7/220°C/fan
oven 200°C. Spray a non stick baking tray with
the cooking spray.

2 To make the topping, spray a non stick saucepan
with the cooking spray and heat until sizzling.
Add the onion and garlic and stir fry for 5 minutes
until softened. Add the turkey mince and cook for
5 minutes over a medium heat until brown. Add the
herbs and tomatoes, reduce the heat and simmer
for 10 minutes. Season.

3 Place the pizza base on the baking tray and
spread the topping over it. Top with tomato slices
and sprinkle with the chilli. Bake for 8–10 minutes
until the base is golden. Cut in half and serve.

Tip…The topping needs to be quite thick so
if it is too runny, cook it for a further 5 minutes.

Variation…Most supermarkets now stock
turkey mince, but as an alternative you can use
140 g (5 oz) (about two) chopped turkey steaks
and the POINTS values will be 3½ per serving.

Linguine ragu

❄ sauce only | **Serves 2** | **10½ POINTS** values per recipe |
Takes 25 minutes to prepare, **15** minutes to cook |
381 calories per serving

> 110 g (4 oz) extra lean beef mince
> 1 onion, sliced
> 2 garlic cloves, crushed
> 2 celery sticks, diced
> 1 carrot, peeled and diced
> 100 ml (3½ fl oz) dry red wine
> 200 g can chopped tomatoes
> ½ beef stock cube, dissolved in
>   100 ml (3½ fl oz) boiling water
> 2 teaspoons dried oregano
> 2 tablespoons tomato purée
> 110 g (4 oz) dried linguine
> salt and freshly ground black pepper

1 Heat a large, non stick frying pan until hot.
Add the beef mince and dry fry for 2–3 minutes
until browned. Remove with a slotted spoon.

2 Add the onion and garlic to the pan and cook
over a medium heat for 5 minutes until softened.
Add the celery and carrot and stir fry for 2 minutes
longer. Add the wine and simmer for another
2–3 minutes to slightly reduce the sauce before
adding the tomatoes, stock, oregano, tomato
purée and beef mince. Simmer for 15 minutes
until slightly thickened. Season.

3 Meanwhile, bring a large pan of water to the
boil, add the pasta and cook for 10–12 minutes
or according to the packet instructions. Drain
and rinse thoroughly. Toss the linguine into the
ragu and mix well before serving.

Variation…Use the same amount of turkey
mince instead of beef mince. The POINTS values
will be 4½ per serving.

Bucatini with meatballs

(4½ POINTS VALUE)

❄ sauce and meatballs only | **Serves 4** | **18½ POINTS**
values per recipe | **Takes 25** minutes to prepare, **1 hour
15** minutes to cook | **325** calories per serving

For the sauce:
low fat cooking spray
1 onion, chopped finely
1 carrot, peeled and chopped finely
1 celery stick, chopped finely
1 red pepper, de-seeded and chopped finely
2 garlic cloves, crushed
a pinch of chilli flakes
2 x 400 g cans chopped tomatoes
*160 g (5¾ oz) dried bucatini or other thick,
    long stranded pasta*

For the meatballs:
300 g (10½ oz) lean steak mince
1 small onion, grated
2 tablespoons chopped fresh flat leaf parsley
1 tablespoon chopped fresh sage
1 tablespoon chopped fresh thyme
1 garlic clove, crushed

1 Spray a medium, lidded, non stick saucepan with
the cooking spray and place over a medium heat.
Add the onion, carrot, celery and red pepper. Cover
and cook over a low heat until softened, for about
15–20 minutes, stirring occasionally.

2 Add the garlic and chilli flakes and cook for a further
minute. Add the tomatoes, bring to the boil and
simmer, covered, for 20 minutes. Remove the lid and
simmer for a further 15 minutes, until slightly thickened.

3 Meanwhile, mix together all the ingredients for
the meatballs. Using moist hands, shape the mixture
into 12 meatballs, each about the size of a walnut.

4 Heat a large, non stick frying pan over a high heat
and spray with the cooking spray. Brown the meatballs,
in batches if necessary, over a medium heat, turning
often then add them to the tomato sauce. Simmer for
a further 20 minutes until cooked through.

5 Meanwhile, bring a large pan of water to the boil
and add the pasta. Cook for 8 minutes, or according
to the packet instructions, until al dente. Drain well.

6 Divide the pasta between four serving plates and
top with the sauce and meatballs.

Meat and poultry 19

Hawaiian pizza

Serves 2 | 9½ *POINTS* values per recipe | Takes 15 minutes | **319** calories per serving

This pizza can be on the table in a matter of minutes.

> 23 cm (9 inch) ready made thin and
>   crispy pizza base
> **For the topping:**
> 3 tablespoons tomato purée
> 110 g (4 oz) wafer thin ham, shredded
> 4 pineapple rings from a tin of pineapple
>   in juice, drained and cut into chunks
> 25 g (1 oz) half fat Cheddar cheese,
>   freshly grated

1 Preheat the oven to Gas Mark 7/220°C/fan oven 200°C.
2 Spread the pizza base with the tomato purée, then top with the ham, pineapple and cheese.
3 Spray a non stick baking tray, put the pizza on it and bake for 8–10 minutes, or following the packet instructions, until the base is golden and the cheese is bubbling.

Tip...For a crispy base, place your pizza directly on to the oven shelf with a baking sheet below to catch any drips.

Variation...Use 110 g (4 oz) Quorn Deli Ham Style Slices instead of the ham for 4½ POINTS values per serving.

Pasta in a paper bag

Serves 4 | 13½ *POINTS* values per recipe | Takes 40 minutes | **248** calories per serving

> low fat cooking spray
> 2 garlic cloves, sliced
> 2 rashers smoked lean back bacon,
>   cut into strips
> 450 g (1 lb) baby plum tomatoes, halved
> 290 g jar roasted peppers in vinegar,
>   drained and sliced
> 4 fresh rosemary sprigs
> 150 ml (5 fl oz) dry white wine
> 4 tablespoons vegetable stock
> 175 g (6 oz) dried spaghetti, broken into
>   approximately 6 cm (2½ inch) pieces
> 10 pitted black olives in brine, halved
> salt and freshly ground black pepper
> 4 lemon wedges, to serve

1 Preheat the oven to Gas Mark 6/200°C/fan oven 180°C. Spray a lidded, non stick frying pan with the cooking spray. Heat until sizzling then add the garlic and bacon and stir fry for 3 minutes until golden. Remove from the pan. Set aside. Spray the pan again, add the tomatoes, peppers and rosemary and cook for 2 minutes. Add the wine and stock, bring to the boil, cover and simmer for 5 minutes until soft. Season.
2 Cut some baking parchment into four pieces, each about 40 cm (16 inch) square and place them on two baking trays. Bring a pan of water to the boil and cook the pasta for half of the cooking time in the packet instructions. Drain thoroughly and mix with the tomato sauce.
3 Divide the mixture between the four pieces of parchment, top with the bacon and garlic mix and the olives. Scrunch up the paper to form a parcel. Bake in the oven for 8 minutes or until the pasta is just cooked. Open one of the parcels to check if the pasta is cooked but beware of the hot steam. Serve each parcel on a plate and let your guests open their own. Serve each with a lemon wedge.

Stuffed tomatoes

Serves 4 | **6½ POINTS** values per recipe | **Takes 25** minutes to prepare, **40** minutes to cook | **129** calories per serving

4 large, firm beef steak tomatoes
low fat cooking spray
2 shallots, diced
1 garlic clove, crushed
110 g (4 oz) extra lean beef mince
1 carrot, peeled and diced into
     1 cm (½ inch) pieces
1 celery stick, sliced into 1 cm (½ inch) pieces
1 tablespoon tomato purée
1 teaspoon dried thyme
50 g (1¾ oz) dried small pasta shapes
salt and freshly ground black pepper

1 Slice the tops off the tomatoes and reserve. Scoop out the insides of the tomatoes and enough flesh so that the shell that remains is about 1 cm (½ inch) thick. Reserve all the insides of the tomatoes for the filling.

2 Preheat the oven to Gas Mark 4/180°C/fan oven 160°C. Spray a non stick saucepan with the cooking spray and heat until sizzling. Add the shallots and garlic and cook, stirring, for 3 minutes. Add the beef and cook, stirring, for a further 5 minutes. Add the carrot, celery, tomato purée, thyme and reserved tomato flesh. Simmer gently for 15 minutes.

3 Meanwhile, bring a pan of water to the boil. Add the pasta and cook for 8 minutes, or according to the packet instructions, then drain and rinse. Mix the pasta with the beef mixture and season.

4 Place the tomatoes in a baking dish and spoon in the beef and pasta mixture. Replace the tomato tops and bake for 25 minutes until the tomatoes are soft.

Chorizo pizza with warm potato salad

Serves 4 | 20½ *POINTS* values per recipe | **Takes 25** minutes to prepare, **35** minutes to cook | **300** calories per serving

    low fat cooking spray
    144 g pack pizza base mix
    For the topping:
    2 onions, sliced
    1 teaspoon fresh rosemary leaves, chopped
    110 g (4 oz) chorizo sausage, chopped into
        2 cm (¾ inch) dice
    10 cherry tomatoes, halved
    For the salad:
    450 g (1 lb) new potatoes, scrubbed and
        chopped if large
    3 tablespoons fat free dressing
    2 tablespoons capers, drained and chopped
    1 tablespoon shredded mint leaves
    salt and freshly ground black pepper

1 Preheat the oven to Gas Mark 7/220°C/fan oven 200°C. Spray a baking tray with the cooking spray and set aside. Prepare the pizza base according to the packet instructions. Make a 24 cm (9½ inch) round, and place it on the baking tray.

2 Spray a non stick frying pan with the cooking spray and heat. Add the onions and stir fry over a medium heat for 5 minutes until softened and beginning to brown. Add a splash of water if it starts to stick. Add the rosemary and cool slightly.

3 Spread the onions over the pizza base, top with the chorizo and tomatoes. Bake for 15–20 minutes until golden.

4 Meanwhile, prepare the salad. Fill a lidded saucepan with water, add the potatoes and bring to the boil. Cover and reduce the heat to simmering and cook for 10–15 minutes until tender. Drain. Mix in the dressing, capers and mint and season. Divide the pizza into four and serve with the salad.

Creamy mushroom and sausage fettuccine

Serves 4 | 15 *POINTS* values per recipe | **Takes 40** minutes | **294** calories per serving

    175 g (6 oz) dried fettuccine
    low fat cooking spray
    4 thin low fat sausages
    450 g (1 lb) mixed mushrooms such as
        chanterelles, girolles and cultivated varieties
        such as chestnut, button or portobello,
        cleaned and halved if large
    2 leeks, cut in rounds
    2 garlic cloves, crushed
    150 ml (5 fl oz) vegetable or chicken stock
    80 g (3 oz) half fat crème fraîche
    2 tablespoons snipped chives
    salt and freshly ground black pepper
    a sprinkling of paprika, to garnish (optional)

1 Bring a large pan of water to the boil, add the pasta and cook for 10–12 minutes or according to the packet instructions. Drain and rinse thoroughly.

2 Meanwhile, spray a large, non stick frying pan with the cooking spray. Add the sausages and cook for 10–15 minutes, turning frequently, until golden all over. Remove from the pan and, when cool enough to handle, cut into chunks.

3 Re-spray the pan with the cooking spray, add the mushrooms, leeks and garlic. Cook for 8 minutes until softened and the juices have evaporated.

4 Stir in the stock, crème fraîche and chives, together with the sausages and season. Reduce the heat and simmer for 2 minutes until hot. Mix in the pasta, heat through and serve garnished with a dusting of paprika, if using.

Tip...The best way to clean mushrooms is to gently wipe each one with a piece of damp kitchen paper. Don't rinse them in water as they'll absorb the water and have less flavour when cooked.

Pancetta pizza

Serves 4 | **26 POINTS** values per recipe | **Takes 25** minutes to prepare, **15–20** minutes to cook | **270** calories per serving

> low fat cooking spray
> 144 g pack pizza base mix
> **For the topping:**
> 130 g (4½ oz) pancetta cubetti, diced
> 150 g (5½ oz) whole baby portobello or
>   closed cap mushrooms, halved
> 1 red pepper, de-seeded and sliced
> 2 garlic cloves, sliced
> 100 g (3½ oz) passata
> 25 g (1 oz) half fat Cheddar cheese,
>   freshly grated

1 Preheat the oven to Gas Mark 7/220°C/fan oven 200°C. Spray a baking tray with the cooking spray and set aside. Mix the dough according to the packet instructions, making 1 large pizza, about 22 cm (8½ inches) in diameter.

2 Heat a large non stick frying pan and dry fry the pancetta over a medium heat for 3–4 minutes until browned. Remove from the pan. Spray the pan with the cooking spray and heat until sizzling. Add the mushrooms and pepper and cook over a medium heat for 5 minutes, add the garlic and cook for a further 2 minutes until the mushroom juices have evaporated. Remove from the heat.

3 Spread the passata over the pizza base, top with the mushroom mixture and pancetta and sprinkle over the cheese. Bake for 15–20 minutes until golden and bubbling. Cut into four and serve.

Variation…Use 150 g (5½ oz) medium skinless chicken breasts, cut into strips, instead of the pancetta. Spray the frying pan with the cooking spray and stir fry for 5 minutes until golden and cooked through, for 3 POINTS values per serving.

Fusilli primavera

Serves 4 | **11 POINTS** values per recipe | **Takes 30** minutes | **236** calories per serving

This traditional springtime dish makes the most of fresh green vegetables from the garden.

> 175 g (6 oz) dried fusilli
> 110 g (4 oz) asparagus tips
> 110 g (4 oz) mange tout, halved
> 110 g (4 oz) green beans, trimmed and halved
> low fat cooking spray
> 1 courgette, diced (about 2 cm/ ¾ inch pieces)
> 1 red pepper, de-seeded and diced
>   (about 1 cm/½ inch)
> 75 g (2¾ oz) wafer thin ham, cut into strips
> 1 tablespoon snipped chives
> finely grated zest of a lemon
> 150 g (5½ oz) virtually fat free fromage frais
> salt and freshly ground black pepper

1 Bring a large pan of water to the boil, add the pasta and cook for 10–12 minutes or according to the packet instructions. Add the asparagus tips, mange tout and green beans for the final 3 minutes of cooking time. Reserving 4 tablespoons of the cooking liquid, drain the pasta and vegetables and rinse thoroughly. Return to the pan, remove from the heat and set aside.

2 Meanwhile, spray a non stick frying pan with the cooking spray. Add the courgette and pepper and stir fry for 5 minutes over a high heat until golden.

3 Add the courgette mixture, ham, chives, lemon zest, fromage frais and reserved cooking liquid to the pasta and vegetables. Return the pan to the heat and cook over a low heat for 2 minutes, stirring frequently until hot. Season and serve.

Ⓥ *Variation*…Use 75 g (2¾ oz) Quorn Deli Ham Style Slices instead of the ham, for 2½ POINTS values per serving.

Balsamic chicken pizza

6 POINTS VALUE

Serves 2 | **11½** *POINTS* values per recipe | **Takes 30** minutes to prepare, **12** minutes to cook | **366** calories per serving

23 cm (9 inch) ready made thin and crispy pizza base
salt and freshly ground black pepper
For the topping:
low fat cooking spray
1 small onion, chopped finely
400 g can cherry tomatoes in juice
1 tablespoon chopped fresh basil leaves
100 g (3½ oz) skinless boneless chicken breast, chopped into 1 cm (½ inch) pieces
2 tablespoons balsamic vinegar
1 yellow pepper, de-seeded and sliced (optional)
75 g (2¾ oz) light mozzarella, drained and torn into pieces
fresh basil leaves, to garnish

1 To make the tomato sauce, spray a medium saucepan with the cooking spray and place over a medium heat. Add the onion and cook for about 5–7 minutes until softened, adding a little water if necessary. Add the tomatoes and basil. Bring to the boil and simmer for 20–25 minutes until thickened. Season and set aside.

2 Preheat the oven to Gas Mark 7/220°C/fan oven 200°C. Meanwhile, put the chicken pieces in a small bowl with 1 tablespoon of the balsamic vinegar and set aside for 10 minutes.

3 Spray a small non stick frying pan with the cooking spray and place over a high heat. Add the chicken and the vinegar marinade. Cook, stirring, for about 3–5 minutes until the chicken is cooked through and most of the vinegar has evaporated. Add the remaining vinegar. Stir to deglaze the pan. Allow the vinegar to reduce for 1–2 minutes until it just coats the chicken and remove from the heat.

4 Spray a non stick baking tray with cooking spray and put the pizza base on it. Spread the pizza base with the tomato sauce. Scatter with the chicken pieces and pepper, if using. Drizzle with any reduced vinegar in the pan and top with the mozzarella. Bake for 10–12 minutes until the base is golden and the cheese is bubbling. Serve immediately, garnished with basil leaves.

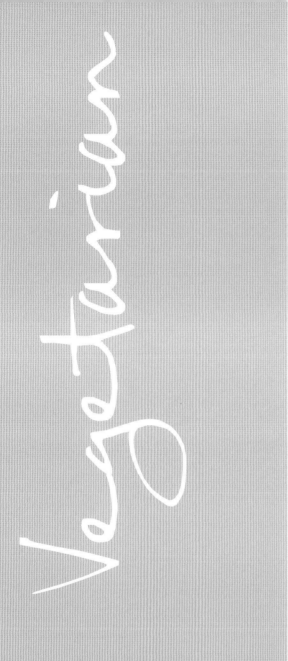

If you're looking for some **inspiring** ways with vegetables, enjoy the deliciously intense flavours of the Roasted Mediterranean Vegetable Pizza or the **comforting simplicity** of Pasta with Pesto Sauce. And for something quick, turn to the Courgette and Rocket Pizza.

Balsamic roasted red onion pizza with feta

4½ POINTS VALUE

Ⓥ **Serves 2** | **8½ POINTS** values per recipe | **Takes 10** minutes to prepare, **45** minutes to cook | **396** calories per serving

> 23 cm (9 inch) ready made thin and crispy
>   pizza base
> **For the topping:**
> 3 red onions, each cut into 6 wedges
> low fat cooking spray
> 4 tablespoons balsamic vinegar
> 3 or 4 bushy fresh thyme sprigs,
>   plus extra to garnish
> 400 g can chopped tomatoes
> 1 garlic clove, crushed
> 75 g (2¾ oz) reduced fat feta cheese,
>   crumbled
> salt and freshly ground black pepper

1 Preheat the oven to Gas Mark 6/200°C/fan oven 180°C. Spread the onion wedges evenly over the base of a large roasting tin. Spray with the cooking spray and drizzle over the balsamic vinegar and 5 tablespoons of water. Scatter over the thyme sprigs and transfer to the oven. Roast for 30 minutes, stirring once or twice, until the onions are tender and the balsamic vinegar and water have been reduced to a sticky coating.

2 Meanwhile, put the chopped tomatoes and garlic in a saucepan and bring to the boil. Season then simmer for 20–25 minutes until thickened.

3 Warm a non stick baking tray in the oven for 2–3 minutes. Remove and spray with the cooking spray. Put the pizza base on the tray and spread over the tomato sauce. Top with the roasted onions (discarding the thyme sprigs) and scatter over the cheese. Bake for 12–15 minutes until the pizza base and cheese are golden. Serve immediately, scattered with a little fresh thyme.

Roasted vegetable pasta salad

🟡 **Serves 4** | **14½** *POINTS* values per recipe | **Takes 15** minutes to prepare, **30** minutes to cook + **30** minutes chilling | **389** calories per serving

- 1 large butternut squash peeled, de-seeded and cut into chunks
- 2 red onions, cut into wedges
- 1 red pepper, de-seeded and cut into chunks
- 1 yellow pepper, de-seeded and cut into chunks
- low fat cooking spray
- 2 teaspoons coriander seeds
- 1 teaspoon cumin seeds
- 250 g (9 oz) dried cavatappi or spiral macaroni

For the dressing:
- 1 tablespoon fat free dressing
- 3 tablespoons 0% fat Greek yogurt
- 1 tablespoon medium curry paste
- 2 tablespoons chopped fresh parsley
- salt and freshly ground black pepper

1 Preheat the oven to Gas Mark 7/220°C/fan oven 200°C. Place all the vegetables in a large roasting tin, in a single layer. Spray with the cooking spray.

2 Heat a dry frying pan until hot. Cook the coriander and cumin seeds over a medium heat for 2 minutes until they pop and their aroma is released, then crush and sprinkle them over the vegetables. Roast for 30 minutes, stirring occasionally, until tender and lightly charred. Remove from the oven and leave to cool.

3 Bring a large pan of water to the boil and add the pasta. Cook for 10–12 minutes or according to the packet instructions. Drain and rinse in plenty of cold water.

4 Mix together the dressing ingredients and pour over the pasta, stirring in the vegetables. Season to taste, cool and chill for 30 minutes to allow the flavours to develop.

Green vegetable pasta

🟡 **Serves 2** | **14½** *POINTS* values per recipe | **Takes 35** minutes | **416** calories per serving

- 50 g (1¾ oz) sugar snap peas, halved lengthways
- 50 g (1¾ oz) green beans, trimmed
- 50 g (1¾ oz) broccoli, broken into small florets
- 50 g (1¾ oz) frozen soya beans, thawed
- 125 g (4½ oz) dried ribbon pasta, e.g. tagliatelle, linguine or pappardelle
- 50 g (1¾ oz) low fat soft cheese
- 125 g (4½ oz) half fat crème fraîche (see Tip)
- zest and juice of ½ a lemon
- 2 tablespoons chopped fresh basil
- salt and freshly ground black pepper

1 Bring a large pan of water to the boil. Add the vegetables. Return the water to the boil and cook for 4 minutes. Using a slotted spoon, remove the vegetables to a colander. Rinse under cold running water, drain well and pat dry on kitchen paper. Set aside.

2 Return the water to the boil and add the pasta. Cook for 8–9 minutes, or according to the packet instructions, until al dente. Drain well. Return the drained pasta to the pan.

3 Meanwhile, in a small saucepan, gently heat together the soft cheese, crème fraîche and lemon zest. Add the vegetables and simmer very gently for about 3–4 minutes until the vegetables are heated through. Remove from the heat and add lemon juice to taste. Stir in the basil and season.

4 Add the vegetable sauce to the pasta and mix well. Divide between two serving plates and serve immediately.

Tip... If you wish, you can use Weight Watchers crème fraîche, for 5 POINTS values per serving.

Spinach and mushroom cannelloni

Serves 4 | **20½ POINTS** values per recipe | **Takes 15** minutes to prepare, **30** minutes to cook | **359** calories per serving

low fat cooking spray
300 g (10½ oz) mushrooms, chopped finely
2 garlic cloves, peeled and crushed
450 g (1 lb) spinach leaves, washed
4 tablespoons tomato purée
2 teaspoons dried thyme
16 cannelloni tubes (about 150 g/5½ oz)
600 ml (20 fl oz) skimmed milk
3 tablespoons cornflour
1 tablespoon coarse grain mustard
75 g (2¾ oz) half fat Cheddar cheese,
    freshly grated
25 g (1 oz) Parmesan cheese, freshly grated
2 tomatoes, sliced
salt and freshly ground black pepper
crisp green salad leaves, to serve

1 Preheat the oven to Gas Mark 6/200°C/fan oven 180°C. Spray a large pan with the cooking spray and when it is hot, add the mushrooms and cook over a medium heat for 3 minutes until the juices begin to flow. Add the garlic and continue cooking for 2 minutes until the juices have evaporated.

2 Add the spinach in batches and cook, stirring until wilted. Remove from the heat and stir in the tomato purée, thyme and seasoning. Cool slightly.

3 Using the end of a teaspoon, stuff the cannelloni tubes with the spinach and mushroom mixture and place in a single layer in a baking dish.

4 Reserving 4 tablespoons of milk, bring the rest to the boil in a saucepan. Blend the cornflour with the reserved milk to make a paste and pour into the pan. While stirring, bring it back to the boil and cook until thickened. It should still be quite runny. Remove the sauce from the heat. Add the mustard and half of each of the Cheddar and Parmesan cheeses. Season.

5 Pour the sauce over the cannelloni, top with the tomato slices and sprinkle with the remaining cheeses. Bake for 30 minutes until golden. Serve four tubes each with crisp green salad leaves.

Margherita pizza

Y | **Serves 2** | **8½ *POINTS*** values per recipe | **Takes 30** minutes + **20** minutes soaking | **323** calories per serving

Sun-dried tomatoes give this classic cheese and tomato pizza a really fabulous tomato flavour.

23 cm (9 inch) ready made thin and crispy
    pizza base
For the topping:
40 g (1½ oz) sun-dried tomatoes
boiling water, for soaking
low fat cooking spray
1 onion, sliced thinly
1 garlic clove, crushed
200 g can chopped tomatoes
1 tablespoon tomato purée
1 tablespoon basil leaves, shredded,
    plus extra to garnish
50 g (1¾ oz) half fat Cheddar cheese,
    freshly grated
salt and freshly ground black pepper

1 Cover the sun-dried tomatoes with boiling water and leave to soak for 20 minutes. Drain then roughly chop.

2 Preheat the oven to Gas Mark 7/220°C/fan oven 200°C. Spray a non stick frying pan with the cooking spray and heat until hot. Add the onion and garlic and cook over a low to medium heat for 10 minutes until softened and just caramelised. Add the chopped tomatoes, tomato purée and sun-dried tomatoes. Simmer for 5 minutes until thick and pulpy. Stir in the basil and seasoning.

3 Warm a non stick baking tray in the oven for 2–3 minutes. Remove and spray with the cooking spray. Place the pizza base on the baking tray, spread it with the tomato sauce and top with the grated cheese. Bake for 8–10 minutes until golden and bubbling.

♥ Variation...Slice 110 g (4 oz) mushrooms and cook with the onion in step 1. The POINTS values per serving will remain the same.

Vegetable pasta stew

Y | **Serves 4** | **19½ *POINTS*** values per recipe | **Takes 35** minutes | **375** calories per serving

This hearty winter stew is packed with root vegetables and a delicious creamy crash.

low fat cooking spray
1 onion, sliced
2 garlic cloves, sliced
200 g (7 oz) turnips, quartered
200 g (7 oz) Chantenay carrots, trimmed
200 g (7 oz) baby parsnips, peeled and trimmed,
    or larger parsnips, peeled and cut into chunks
150 g (5½ oz) mushrooms, halved
200 g (7 oz) dried conchiglie or shell pasta
700 ml (1¼ pts) hot vegetable stock
125 ml (4 fl oz) dry red wine
2 rosemary sprigs
4 thyme sprigs
2 bay leaves
400 g can borlotti beans, drained and rinsed
110 g (4 oz) green beans, chopped
2 tablespoons half fat crème fraîche

1 Spray a large, lidded saucepan with the cooking spray. Heat over a medium heat until sizzling, then add the onion and garlic. Cook for 5 minutes until softened, adding a splash of water if it starts to stick. Add the turnips, carrots, parsnips and mushrooms. Cook, stirring, for 5 minutes until just beginning to brown.

2 Add the pasta, stock, red wine and herbs. Bring to the boil, cover and simmer for 10 minutes, stirring occasionally.

3 Add the beans. Cook for 5 minutes until all the vegetables are tender and the pasta is cooked. Remove the bay leaves and stir in the crème fraîche. Bring back to the boil to heat then serve.

Tip...If you want a lighter stew, omit the crème fraîche for 4 POINTS values per serving.

Pasta with pesto sauce

Serves 4 | **15½ POINTS** values per recipe | **Takes 20 minutes** | **255** calories per serving

20 g (¾ oz) pine nut kernels
40 g (1½ oz) fresh basil leaves
2 tablespoons extra virgin olive oil
175 g (6 oz) dried spaghetti, linguine
    or tagliatelle
salt and freshly ground black pepper

1 Heat a small non stick frying pan until hot, add the pine nut kernels and dry fry over a medium heat for 1–2 minutes, stirring until golden all over. Place the basil, olive oil, pine nut kernels and a pinch of salt in a food processor or liquidiser and blend briefly to a paste.

2 Bring a large pan of water to the boil, add the pasta and cook for 10–12 minutes or according to the packet instructions. Reserve 4 tablespoons of cooking liquid. Drain and rinse thoroughly. Return the pasta to the pan with the pesto sauce and reserved cooking liquid. Stir through, season and serve immediately.

Tip ...The heat from the **pasta** is enough to warm the pesto. The pesto will keep, covered, in the fridge for a week.

Variation... Make a basil and roasted pepper pesto by adding two drained and chopped roasted **peppers** in vinegar to the blender. The POINTS values will remain the same.

Courgette and rocket pizza

🌱 **Serves 4** | **17 *POINTS*** values per recipe | **Takes 15** minutes to prepare + **30** minutes proving, **10–20** minutes to cook | **216** calories per serving

Smoked paprika gives this pizza something special and it goes so well with the creamy courgettes and peppery rocket. It is hotter than normal paprika.

For the pizza base:
140 g (5 oz) strong white flour,
    with 2 teaspoons reserved for dusting
1 teaspoon smoked paprika
½ teaspoon instant dried yeast
a pinch of salt
For the topping:
low fat cooking spray
1 large courgette, cubed
1 garlic clove, chopped
2 tablespoons sun-dried tomato purée
3 tomatoes, sliced
125 g (4½ oz) light mozzarella,
    drained and sliced
salt and freshly ground pepper
25 g (1 oz) wild rocket, to garnish

1 Place the flour in a large bowl and stir in the paprika, yeast and salt. Add 7–8 tablespoons of hand hot water and mix it in. It's easiest to do this with a wooden spoon to start with and then use your hands.

2 Sprinkle the reserved flour on to a clean work surface. Once the dough has come together and no longer clings to the sides of the bowl, turn it out on to the lightly floured surface. Knead the dough for at least 5 minutes until it is soft and stretchy. Roll out the dough to 24 cm (9½ inches).

3 Spray a non stick baking tray with the cooking spray. Place the dough on the baking tray and cover with a clean cloth. Leave in a warm, draught free place to prove until doubled in size, about 20–30 minutes or a little longer if not yet doubled after this time.

4 Preheat the oven to Gas Mark 7/220°C/fan oven 200°C. Spray a non stick frying pan with the cooking spray and heat. Add the courgette and garlic and fry over a high heat for 3–4 minutes, stirring occasionally until browned.

5 Spread the tomato purée over the pizza base, top with the tomato slices, courgettes and mozzarella. Season and bake for 10–20 minutes until golden and bubbling. Serve garnished with rocket.

Tip... Don't stir the courgettes too much; each side needs to have time to brown.

Pasta omelette

Serves 2 | **9 POINTS** values per recipe | **Takes 30** minutes | **304** calories per serving

Serve with some **tomatoes**, **red onion** rings and half a sliced **chilli**. Drizzle with 1 teaspoon of balsamic vinegar and fat free dressing.

75 g (2¾ oz) dried penne
1 tablespoon pesto
low fat cooking spray
a bunch of spring onions, *chopped*
3 eggs, *beaten*
1 tablespoon chopped fresh parsley
1 teaspoon dried thyme
1 tablespoon chopped chives
2 egg whites
salt and freshly ground black pepper

1 Bring a large pan of water to the boil, add the pasta and cook according to the packet instructions. Drain and rinse thoroughly. Stir in the pesto.

2 Spray a non stick frying pan with the cooking spray and heat over a medium heat until sizzling. Add the spring onions and cook for 5 minutes until just beginning to brown.

3 Add the spring onions to the beaten eggs along with the herbs and pasta. In a separate bowl, whisk the egg whites until stiff, then carefully fold them into the pasta mixture and season. Pour this mixture into the frying pan. Cook for 6–7 minutes until set.

4 Invert a plate over the top of the frying pan. Turn the whole thing upside down so that the omelette is brown side up on the plate, then carefully slide the omelette back into the pan. Cook for 2 minutes more to brown the underneath. Alternatively, if using an ovenproof pan, grill the top of the omelette under a preheated medium grill for 3 minutes until golden. Divide in two and serve.

Variation...Replace the **spring onions** with 1 sliced **courgette**, and cook as in step 2. The POINTS values per serving will be the same.

Roasted tomato spaghetti

Serves 4 | **21 POINTS** values per recipe | **Takes 25** minutes | **320** calories per serving

Don't be put off by the amount of garlic in this recipe, when roasted, the cloves become sweet and lose their pungency.

low fat cooking spray
750 g (1 lb 10 oz) cherry tomatoes
8 garlic cloves
2 teaspoons extra virgin olive oil
225 g (8 oz) dried spaghetti
4 tablespoons shredded basil *leaves*
2 tablespoons balsamic vinegar
125 g pack light mozzarella, drained
*   and chopped roughly*
salt and freshly ground black pepper

1 Preheat the oven to Gas Mark 7/220°C/fan oven 200°C. Line a roasting tin with foil and spray with the cooking spray. Place the tomatoes and garlic in the tin, drizzle with the olive oil, swirling the tin around to coat the tomatoes and roast for 20 minutes until the tomatoes are just charred and split.

2 Meanwhile, bring a large pan of water to the boil, add the pasta and cook for 10–12 minutes or according to the packet instructions. Drain and rinse thoroughly.

3 Remove the garlic cloves from the roasting tin and set them aside to cool slightly. Mix the tomatoes, pasta and basil together in the tin, season and reheat.

4 Squeeze the garlic from its skin – it will be quite soft – and mix with the balsamic vinegar. Stir the garlic mixture into the pasta with the chopped mozzarella. Leave it for 2 minutes so that the heat melts the mozzarella then serve.

Variation...Omit the mozzarella and serve sprinkled with 2 tablespoons of freshly grated Parmesan cheese, for 4 POINTS values per serving.

Roasted Mediterranean vegetable pizza

Ⓥ ❋ sauce only | **Serves 2** | **7 POINTS** values per recipe |
Takes 35 minutes to prepare + **30** minutes proving,
55 minutes to cook | **280** calories per serving

This classic medley of roasted Mediterranean
vegetables is a real crowd pleaser.

For the pizza base:
70 g (2½ oz) strong white flour, with
    1 teaspoon reserved for dusting
¼ teaspoon instant dried yeast
a pinch of salt
low fat cooking spray
For the sauce:
½ onion, chopped finely
1 garlic clove, crushed
200 g can chopped tomatoes
1 tablespoon finely chopped fresh basil
salt and freshly ground black pepper
For the topping:
1 small courgette, cut into chunky slices
    crosswise at an angle
1 small red onion, cut into 8 wedges
1 red pepper, de-seeded and cut into
    quarters, lengthwise
1 small aubergine, cut into
    2.5 cm (1 inch) chunks
2 canned artichoke hearts, drained
    and quartered
50 g (1¾ oz) light mozzarella, drained
    and torn into pieces

1 Place the flour in a large bowl and stir in the yeast
and salt. Add 3–4 tablespoons of hand hot water
and mix in. It's easiest to do this with a wooden
spoon to start with and then use your hands.

2 Sprinkle the reserved flour on to a clean work
surface. Once the dough has come together and no
longer clings to the sides of the bowl, turn it out on
to the lightly floured surface. Knead the dough for
at least 5 minutes until it is soft and stretchy.

3 Spray a non stick baking tray with the cooking
spray. Place the dough on the baking tray and cover
with a clean cloth. Leave in a warm, draft free place
to prove until doubled in size, about 20–30 minutes
or a little longer if not yet doubled after this time.
Roll out the dough to a 24 cm (9½ inch) circle.

4 Meanwhile, make the sauce. Spray a medium
saucepan with the cooking spray and place over
a medium heat. Add the onion and cook for
5–7 minutes until softened, adding a little water
if it starts to stick. Add the garlic and cook for a
further 30 seconds before adding the tomatoes
and basil. Season, bring to the boil and simmer
for 15–20 minutes, until thickened. Set aside.

5 Preheat the oven to Gas Mark 7/220°C/fan
oven 200°C. For the topping, put all the prepared
vegetables except the artichokes into a large shallow
roasting tray and spray with the cooking spray. Roast
for 30–40 minutes, stirring once or twice, until all the
vegetables are tender and charred at the edges.

6 Spread the dough with the tomato sauce, scatter
over the roasted vegetables and artichokes and dot
with the cheese. Transfer to the oven and bake for
12–15 minutes until the pizza base is golden and the
cheese is bubbling. Serve immediately.

Mixed tomato pizza

Serves 4 | **16 POINTS** values per recipe | **Takes 10** minutes to prepare + **30** minutes proving, **15** minutes to cook | **204** calories per serving

For the pizza base:
140 g (5 oz) strong white flour, with
    2 teaspoons reserved for dusting
½ teaspoon instant dried yeast
a pinch of salt

For the topping:
25 g (1 oz) sun-dried tomatoes
boiling water, for soaking
400 g (14 oz) mixed tomatoes, including
    red, orange and yellow cherry tomatoes,
    plum tomatoes and vine tomatoes
low fat cooking spray
125 g pack light mozzarella, drained and
    torn into pieces
salt and freshly ground black pepper
a handful of fresh basil leaves, to garnish

1 Place the flour in a large bowl and stir in the yeast and salt. Add 7–8 tablespoons of hand hot water and mix in. It's easiest to do this with a wooden spoon to start with and then use your hands.

2 Sprinkle the reserved flour on to a clean work surface. Once the dough has come together and no longer clings to the sides of the bowl, turn it out on to the lightly floured surface. Knead the dough for at least 5 minutes until it is soft and stretchy. Divide into two equal balls. Shape the dough into two 25 cm (10 inch) ovals.

3 Cover the sun-dried tomatoes with boiling water and leave to soak for 20 minutes. Drain then slice thinly lengthwise. Spray two non stick baking trays with the cooking spray. Place the dough on the trays and cover with a clean cloth. Leave in a warm, draught free place to prove until doubled in size, about 20–30 minutes or a little longer if not yet doubled after this time. Preheat the oven to Gas Mark 7/220°C/fan oven 200°C.

4 Cut the cherry tomatoes in half and slice the plum tomatoes thinly lengthwise. Slice the vine tomatoes thinly crosswise.

5 Divide all the tomato slices between the pizza bases then scatter with the cherry tomatoes and mozzarella cheese and season. Bake for 12–15 minutes, swapping the trays around in the oven halfway through the cooking time. Cut each pizza base in half and serve scattered with the basil leaves.

Spaghetti with smoked salmon and dill

(4 POINTS VALUE)

Serves 2 | **8½ POINTS** values per recipe | **Takes 15** minutes | **313** calories per serving

Smoked salmon in a creamy ribbons lemon sauce is a really quick and easy treat.

125 g (4½ oz) dried spaghetti
60 g (2 oz) runner beans, *cut into*
    2 cm (¾ inch) pieces
60 g (2 oz) smoked salmon, *cut into*
    3 cm (1¼ inch) strips
150 g (5½ oz) virtually fat free fromage frais
1 tablespoon roughly chopped fresh dill *or*
    1 teaspoon dried dill
finely grated zest of ½ a lemon, plus
    wedges, to serve
salt and freshly ground black pepper

1 Bring a large pan of water to the boil, add the pasta and cook for 10–12 minutes or according to the packet instructions, adding the beans for the final 5 minutes cooking time. Reserve 2 tablespoons of cooking liquid. Drain and rinse thoroughly, then return to the pan.

2 Add the smoked salmon, fromage frais, half the dill, lemon zest and reserved cooking liquid to the pasta mixture. Stir to mix.

3 Heat over a medium heat, stirring for 1 minute until hot, but no longer, to prevent curdling. Divide between two plates, sprinkle with the remaining dill. Serve with a lemon wedge each and black pepper.

Tip ...Packs of **smoked salmon** trimmings are ideal for this dish and very economical.

Variation ...Try adding 60 g (2 oz) cooked, peeled **prawns** for an extra treat, for 4 POINTS values per serving. Add them after step 1 and heat for 2 minutes.

Once you've tried these easy ideas for fish, you'll be hooked. **Enjoy tried and tested favourites** such as Pizza Marinara and Puttanesca Pasta. Discover some exciting new combinations too, such as Spaghetti with Smoked Salmon and Dill.

Pesto prawn pizza

✳ sauce only | **Serves 4** | **23½ POINTS** values per recipe |
Takes 20 minutes to prepare, **45** minutes to cook |
363 calories per serving

2 x 23 cm (9 inch) ready made thin and
    crispy pizza bases
For the tomato sauce:
low fat cooking spray
1 small onion, chopped finely
400 g can chopped tomatoes
1 teaspoon dried oregano
½ teaspoon dried thyme
For the topping:
200 g (7 oz) baby spinach, washed
200 g (7 oz) cooked peeled prawns
2 tablespoons reduced fat pesto
1 yellow pepper, de-seeded and sliced
    thinly crosswise into rings
50 g (1¾ oz) ricotta cheese
100 g (3½ oz) light mozzarella, drained
    and torn into pieces

1 Spray a medium, non stick saucepan with the cooking spray and place over a medium heat. Add the onion and cook for 5–7 minutes until softened, adding a little water if needed. Add the tomatoes, oregano and thyme. Bring to the boil. Simmer for 20–30 minutes until thickened.

2 Put the spinach in a large saucepan. Over a high heat, stir constantly until wilted. Allow to cool then squeeze out as much water as possible. Set aside.

3 In a small bowl, mix together the prawns and pesto. Spray a large, non stick frying pan with the cooking spray and place over a high heat. Add the pepper rings. Cook for 3–4 minutes until softened.

4 Preheat the oven to Gas Mark 7/220°C/fan oven 200°C. Spray a non stick baking tray with cooking spray and put the pizza bases on it. Spread each with half of the tomato sauce. Divide the spinach, prawns and pepper evenly between the bases. Dot with the pesto and ricotta and scatter over the mozzarella. Bake for 12–15 minutes until the cheese is bubbling.

Seafood pasta

Serves 4 | 18½ *POINTS* values per recipe | **Takes 30** minutes | **450** calories per serving

150 g (5½ oz) dried spiral shaped macaroni
(cavatappi or corkscrew)
low fat cooking spray
4 shallots, sliced
2 garlic cloves, crushed
2 tomatoes, de-seeded and diced
125 ml (4 fl oz) dry white wine
1 kg (2 lb 4 oz) mussels, cleaned (see Tip)
250 g (9 oz) peeled, cooked prawns
155 g jar cockles in vinegar, drained
salt and freshly ground black pepper
To serve:
3 tablespoons chopped fresh parsley
4 lemon wedges

1 Bring a large pan of water to the boil, add the pasta and cook according to the packet instructions. Drain and rinse thoroughly.

2 Spray a large, lidded pan with the cooking spray and heat until hot. Add the shallots and cook over a medium heat for 5 minutes until softened, adding a splash of water if they start to stick. Add the garlic and tomatoes and cook for 1 minute.

3 Add the wine and 150 ml (5 fl oz) water with the mussels. Bring to the boil, cover and cook for 2–3 minutes until the mussels have opened. Discard any that have not opened. Add the prawns, cockles and pasta. Heat through for 2 minutes until piping hot. Season to taste, sprinkle over the parsley and serve with the lemon wedges.

Tip...To clean **mussels**, soak them in cold water for 5 minutes and discard any that don't close when tapped. Scrub the shells clean and pull out any hair-like strands (beards) between the shells.

Variation...Add 2 tablespoons of tomato puree with the white wine for a richer tomato sauce. The POINTS values will remain the same.

Smoked haddock pasta

Serves 4 | 19½ *POINTS* values per recipe | **Takes 35** minutes | **381** calories per serving

225 g (8 oz) dried pappardelle
175 g (6 oz) green beans, halved
140 g (5 oz) cauliflower florets
400 g (14 oz) skinless smoked haddock
450 ml (16 fl oz) skimmed milk
1 thyme sprig
1 bay leaf
4 peppercorns
2 tablespoons cornflour
finely grated zest of a lemon
2 tablespoons chopped fresh dill,
or 1 tablespoon dried dill
freshly ground black pepper

1 Bring a large pan of water to the boil, add the pasta and cook for 10–12 minutes or according to the packet instructions, adding the beans and cauliflower for the final 5 minutes of cooking time. Drain and rinse thoroughly.

2 Put the fish in a large, lidded, deep saucepan (you may need to cut the fish to make it fit). Pour over the milk and add the thyme, bay leaf and peppercorns. Bring slowly to the boil, cover and simmer for 10 minutes until the fish just flakes. Drain, reserving the cooking liquid, and remove the herbs and peppercorns.

3 Flake the fish into large chunks, removing any obvious bones, and mix with the pasta and vegetables. Bring the reserved cooking liquid to the boil in a small pan. Blend the cornflour with a tablespoon of cold water, add to the pan and stir in. Return to the boil, stirring until thickened. Cook for 1 minute and stir in the lemon zest and dill. Season with pepper and toss into the pasta mixture.

Variation...Use the same amount of **cod** instead of **haddock** for the same POINTS values per serving.

Tuna Salsa with Fettuccine

Serves 2 | **9½ POINTS** values per recipe | Takes 25 minutes | **369** calories per serving

The succulent and meaty texture of **tuna** lends itself well to Mediterranean flavours.

> 75 g (2¾ oz) dried fettuccine
> 100 g (3½ oz) green beans, halved
> 2 x 110 g (4 oz) tuna steaks
> low fat cooking spray
> 6 spring onions, trimmed
> 6 black olives in brine, drained and halved
> 180 g jar hot salsa dip
> 2 tablespoons chopped fresh coriander

1 Bring a large pan of water to the boil, add the pasta and cook for 10–12 minutes or according to the packet instructions. Add the beans for the last 5 minutes of the cooking time. Drain and rinse thoroughly.

2 Heat a griddle pan until really hot. Spray both sides of the tuna with the cooking spray and cook for 1–2 minutes on each side until browned and cooked through. Remove the tuna and cut into slices. Spray the spring onions with the cooking spray and cook in the griddle pan for 1 minute on each side until softened. Set aside.

3 Mix the olives and salsa dip into the pasta with the sliced tuna and cook over a medium heat for 1–2 minutes until hot. Serve garnished with the spring onions and coriander.

Variations...Try with the same amount of **cod**, flaked into the sauce, instead of **tuna**. The POINTS values will be 3½ per serving. ...Instead of the salsa dip, use 4 tablespoons of reduced fat pesto sauce and the POINTS values will be 5½ per serving.

Pizza party nibbles

Makes 16 | **14½ POINTS** values per recipe | Takes 10 minutes | **53** calories per serving

These very tasty canapés are so low in **POINTS** values that you can afford to indulge a little.

> 140 g (5 oz) asparagus spears (about 16), trimmed and halved lengthways
> 8 (30 g/1¼ oz) mini round pitta breads, halved
> 2 tablespoons tomato purée
> 200 g pack low fat soft cheese
> zest of a lime, grated finely
> 75 g (2¾ oz) smoked salmon, cut into thin strips
> 4 spring onions, chopped finely
> salt and freshly ground black pepper
> 1 lime, cut into wedges, to garnish

1 Preheat the grill to medium. Bring a large pan of water to the boil, add the asparagus spears and cook for 3 minutes until just tender. Drain and rinse with cold water. Set aside.

2 Toast the pitta breads under the grill for 2 minutes, turning once, until warm. Spread each with a little tomato purée.

3 Mix the soft cheese with the lime zest and seasoning. Spoon a teaspoon of this mixture on to each pitta half, then top with the smoked salmon and asparagus spears. Garnish with the spring onions. Serve with lime wedges to squeeze over.

Tip...Get everything ready before you toast the pitta breads so you can serve them when they are still warm.

Variation...Try with 110 g (4 oz) chicken tikka pieces, cut into small strips, instead of the **asparagus** and **smoked salmon** for the same POINTS values per serving.

Puttanesca pasta

❄ sauce only | **Serves 4** | **12 POINTS** values per recipe | **Takes 25** minutes | **214** calories per serving

This classic **pasta** sauce was once made by 'ladies of the night' to woo customers.

175 g (6 oz) dried tagliatelle
1 teaspoon vegetable oil
50 g (1¾ oz) anchovies, rinsed and
    chopped roughly
2 garlic cloves, peeled and crushed
10 black olives in brine, drained and halved
2 tablespoons capers, drained
400 g tin chopped tomatoes
1 tablespoon chopped fresh oregano leaves,
    plus extra to garnish or 2 teaspoons dried
salt and freshly ground black pepper

1 Bring a large pan of water to the boil, add the pasta and cook for 10–12 minutes or according to the packet instructions. Drain and rinse thoroughly.
2 Meanwhile, heat the oil in a saucepan, add the anchovies and cook, stirring, over a medium heat for 3 minutes. Add the garlic and cook for a further 3 minutes until the anchovies have virtually dissolved.
3 Add the olives, capers, tomatoes and oregano. Bring to the boil, reduce the heat and simmer for 5 minutes until thick. Season to taste.
4 Pour the sauce over the pasta and toss to mix. Garnish with extra oregano leaves, if you like.

Tuna and baby corn spaghetti bake

Serves 2 | **9½ POINTS** values per recipe | **Takes 20** minutes to prepare, **30** minutes to cook | **375** calories per serving

75 g (2¾ oz) dried spaghetti,
    broken into pieces
400 g can chopped tomatoes
low fat cooking spray
140 g (5 oz) baby corn, halved
2 garlic cloves, sliced
300 ml (10 fl oz) skimmed milk
1 tablespoon cornflour
185 g can tuna in brine or spring water,
    drained
2 tablespoons capers, rinsed
2 tablespoons chopped fresh parsley
25 g (1 oz) half fat Cheddar cheese,
    freshly grated
salt and freshly ground black pepper

1 Preheat the oven to Gas Mark 5/190°C/fan oven 170°C. Put the broken pasta in the base of a 2 litre (3½ pint) baking dish. Pour over the canned tomatoes and season.
2 Spray a non stick frying pan with the cooking spray and heat. When it is hot, add the baby corn and stir fry for 3 minutes. Add the garlic and continue cooking for 2 minutes. Remove from the heat and set aside.
3 Reserve 2 tablespoons of milk and bring the rest to the boil in a saucepan. Blend the reserved milk with the cornflour and pour into the pan. Cook until thickened, stirring continuously. Stir in the baby corn, garlic, tuna, capers and parsley and season. Pour the sauce over the spaghetti. Sprinkle the cheese on top, put the dish on a baking tray and bake for 30 minutes until golden and bubbling.

Variation...Use a 170 g can of **crab meat** instead of **tuna** for 4½ POINTS values per serving.

Pizza marinara

Serves 4 | 15½ *POINTS* values per recipe | **Takes 20** minutes to prepare + **30** minutes proving, **12–15** minutes to cook | **266** calories per serving

For the pizza base:
140 g (5 oz) strong white flour,
    with 2 teaspoons reserved for dusting
½ teaspoon instant dried yeast
a pinch of salt
For the topping:
low fat cooking spray
1 onion, sliced thinly
1 garlic clove, crushed
400 g can chopped tomatoes
1 tablespoon tomato purée
2 teaspoons dried mixed herbs
200 g (7 oz) peeled, cooked prawns
185 g can tuna in brine or spring water, drained
50 g (1¾ oz) half fat Cheddar cheese, freshly grated
salt and freshly ground black pepper
25 g (1 oz) caper berries, to serve (optional)

1 Place the flour in a large bowl and stir in the yeast and salt. Add 7–8 tablespoons of hand hot water and mix in. It's easiest to do this with a wooden spoon to start with and then use your hands.

2 Sprinkle the reserved flour on to a clean work surface. Once the dough has come together and no longer clings to the sides of the bowl, turn it out on to the lightly floured surface. Knead the dough for at least 5 minutes until it is soft and stretchy. Roll out the dough to a 24 cm (9½ inch) circle.

3 Spray a non stick baking tray with the cooking spray. Place the dough on the tray and cover it with a clean cloth. Leave in a warm, draught free place to prove until doubled in size, about 20–30 minutes or a little longer if not yet doubled after this time. Preheat the oven to Gas Mark 7/220°C/fan oven 200°C.

4 Spray a saucepan with the cooking spray and heat until sizzling. Add the onion and cook over a medium heat for 5 minutes until softened. Add a splash of water if it starts to stick. Add the garlic and tomatoes and simmer for 5 minutes. Stir in the tomato purée, herbs and seasoning.

5 Spread the sauce over the pizza base, top with the prawns and tuna and sprinkle with the cheese. Bake for 12–15 minutes until golden. Top with the caper berries to serve, if using.

Pasta with cullen skink sauce

Serves 4 | **16½** *POINTS* values per recipe | **Takes 30** minutes | **296** calories per serving

> *low fat cooking spray*
> *1 large leek, sliced thinly*
> *1 small onion, chopped finely*
> *300 ml (10 fl oz) skimmed milk*
> *250 g (9 oz) smoked haddock fillet*
> *2 tablespoons sauce flour*
> *2 tablespoons low fat crème fraîche*
> *1 tablespoon finely chopped fresh parsley*
> *160 g (5¾ oz) dried pasta shapes,*
> *   such as penne*
> *salt and freshly ground black pepper*

1 Spray a medium saucepan with the cooking spray, place over a medium heat and add the leek and onion. Cook for 10–12 minutes, adding a little water if they start to stick, until softened.

2 Meanwhile, put the milk in a large, lidded frying pan, bring to the boil then add the haddock. Return to the boil then remove from the heat, cover and leave to stand for 5 minutes. Remove the fish and reserve the milk. Skin the fish and break the flesh into flakes, removing and discarding any bones. Set aside.

3 When the leek and onion have softened, stir in the sauce flour. Gradually add the milk from the cooked fish, stirring continuously. Bring gradually to the simmer, stirring continuously again. Simmer for 2 minutes. Stir in the crème fraîche then add the flaked fish, parsley and seasoning.

4 Meanwhile, bring a large pan of water to the boil and add the pasta. Cook for 8–9 minutes, or according to the packet instructions, until al dente. Drain well.

5 Add the pasta to the sauce and stir well to mix. Divide between four serving dishes and serve immediately.

Spicy crab pasta salad

Serves 2 | **8½** *POINTS* values per recipe | **Takes 20** minutes | **293** calories per serving

This delicious **pasta** salad with a creamy dressing and spicy salsa is ideal for lunch or picnics.

> **For the salsa:**
> *4 spring onions, trimmed and sliced finely*
> *2 tomatoes, de-seeded and diced*
> *1 small red chilli, de-seeded and diced*
> *finely grated zest and juice of a lime*
> *1 tablespoon roughly chopped fresh*
> *   coriander leaves*
> **For the pasta:**
> *110 g (4 oz) dried fusilli*
> *170 g can crab meat in brine, drained*
> *1 tablespoon light salad cream*
> *3 tablespoons 0% fat Greek yogurt*
> *1 teaspoon paprika*
> *salt and freshly ground black pepper*

1 Mix the salsa ingredients together and set aside to allow the flavours to develop.

2 Bring a large pan of water to the boil, add the pasta and cook for 10–12 minutes or according to the packet instructions. Drain and rinse with cold water.

3 Mix the crab, salad cream, yogurt, paprika and seasoning into the pasta. Serve the salsa alongside or mixed in if you prefer.

Tip…Try using **crab sticks** instead of the **crab**. Shred eight crab sticks and mix into the pasta with the dressing, for the same POINTS values per serving. Crab sticks are available from most supermarket fish counters.

4 ½ POINTS VALUE

Quick and Easy

French bread pizza

Serves 4 | 16½ *POINTS* values per recipe | **Takes 10** minutes | **284** calories per serving

French bread is an instant base for pizza so this recipe is ideal for an easy lunch or light supper.

200 g pack **low fat soft cheese with garlic and herbs**
2 tablespoons reduced fat pesto
4 x 60 g (2 oz) pieces French stick, sliced in half lengthways
150 g (5½ oz) cherry tomatoes, halved
390 g can artichokes, drained and quartered
low fat cooking spray
12 basil leaves

1 Preheat the grill to medium. Mix the soft cheese and pesto together and spread over the bread. Place on the grill pan. Top with the cherry tomatoes and artichokes and spray with the cooking spray.
2 Grill for 2–3 minutes until golden and bubbling and serve garnished with basil leaves.

Tip…This is a great way to use up day old French bread.

Turn to delicious and healthy meals such as Grilled Teriyaki Salmon and Pasta or Fiorentina Crumpet Pizza when you need a hand in the kitchen – most of these recipes are ready in **20 minutes or less**.

Penne with watercress sauce

Serves 2 | **5½ POINTS** values per recipe | **Takes 20** minutes | **234** calories per serving

Whizz up this vibrant and nutritious meal in just a few minutes.

> 110 g (4 oz) penne
> low fat cooking spray
> 2 garlic cloves, crushed
> 200 g bag watercress, thick stalks removed
> 2 teaspoons balsamic vinegar
> 2 tomatoes, de-seeded and diced
> salt and freshly ground black pepper
> 2 tablespoons snipped chives, to garnish

1 Bring a large pan of water to the boil, add the pasta and cook for 10–12 minutes or according to the packet instructions. Drain and rinse thoroughly.
2 Meanwhile, heat a large, non stick pan and spray with the cooking spray. Add the garlic and cook over a medium heat for 2 minutes, then add the watercress and cook for 1–2 minutes until just wilted. Transfer to a food processor or liquidiser, add the balsamic vinegar and 1 tablespoon of hot water. Whizz for 1 minute until smooth.
3 Return to the pan with the pasta, add the tomatoes and toss to mix. Season and serve garnished with the chives.

Variation…Mix a 165 g (5¾ oz) skinless chicken breast, cooked and sliced, into the sauce for a *POINTS* value of 4 per serving.

Chorizo and courgette lumache

Serves 4 | **18 POINTS** values per recipe | **Takes 25** minutes | **299** calories per serving

Spicy chorizo sausage complements the creamy courgettes perfectly.

> 225 g (8 oz) dried lumache or any other shell pasta
> 2 courgettes, sliced into ribbons
> 110 g (4 oz) chorizo sausage, cut into 2.5 cm (1 inch) dice
> 200 g (7 oz) field or flat mushrooms, sliced
> 400 g can chopped tomatoes
> 2 tablespoons tomato purée
> 2 teaspoons Tabasco (optional)

1 Bring a large pan of water to the boil, add the pasta and cook for 10–12 minutes or according to the packet instructions, adding the courgette ribbons for the final 2 minutes of cooking. Drain and rinse thoroughly.
2 Heat a large, heavy based frying pan until hot, add the chorizo sausage and dry fry for 3 minutes until the fat begins to run. Add the mushrooms and stir fry over a medium heat for 5 minutes. Add the chopped tomatoes and tomato purée. Bring to the boil and simmer for 5 minutes until thickened slightly.
3 Stir in the Tabasco sauce, if using.
4 Add the sauce to the pasta and cook for 2 minutes until heated through, then serve.

Tip…An easy way to create courgette ribbons is to cut long, thin pieces along the length of the courgette with a potato or vegetable peeler.

Courgette, pesto and lemon pasta

Ⓥ **Serves 1** | **7 POINTS** values per recipe | **Takes 15** minutes | 302 calories per serving

½ tablespoon pine nut kernels
40 g (1½ oz) dried spirali
low fat cooking spray
1 courgette, sliced thinly
a pinch of chilli flakes
25 g (1 oz) sun-dried tomatoes in oil,
    drained and chopped roughly
2 teaspoons red pesto
zest of ½ a lemon
½ tablespoon finely grated Parmesan cheese
salt and freshly ground black pepper

1 Dry fry the pine nut kernels in a non stick frying pan for 2–3 minutes until golden and toasted. Bring a large pan of water to the boil and add the pasta. Cook for 8–9 minutes, or according to the packet instructions, until al dente. Drain well.

2 Meanwhile, spray a non stick frying pan with the cooking spray and place over a high heat. Add the courgette slices and cook for 4–5 minutes until golden. Add the chilli flakes and cook briefly.

3 Return the pasta to the pan and add the courgette slices, sun-dried tomatoes, pine nut kernels, pesto and lemon zest. Season to taste and stir well.

4 Transfer to a serving plate and sprinkle with the cheese. Serve immediately.

Grilled teriyaki salmon and pasta

Serves 1 | 5 *POINTS* values per recipe | Takes 20 minutes + marinating | **411** calories per serving

Teriyaki is a Japanese marinade made from soy sauce, wine, **garlic** and spices. It's great for flavouring **fish**, **chicken** and **vegetables** – what's more, it has zero ***POINTS*** values.

> 100 g (3½ oz) salmon fillet
> 2 tablespoons teriyaki marinade
> 40 g (1½ oz) quick cook spaghetti
> 60 g (2 oz) long stemmed broccoli or florets
> 2 tomatoes, halved
> 1 tablespoon chopped fresh coriander leaves
> zest and juice of ½ a lime, grated finely

1 Place the salmon in a non-metallic bowl. Pour over 1 tablespoon of the teriyaki marinade, cover and leave to marinate for at least 10 minutes.

2 Bring a large pan of water to the boil, add the pasta and cook for 6–8 minutes or according to the packet instructions. Add the broccoli for the final 4 minutes of cooking time. Drain and rinse thoroughly.

3 Preheat the grill to medium and line the grill pan with foil. Brush the tomatoes with the remaining teriyaki marinade and place on the grill pan with the salmon. Grill for 8 minutes, turning halfway through, until golden and the salmon just flakes.

4 Mix the coriander leaves, lime zest and juice into the pasta and broccoli mixture and serve topped with the salmon and tomatoes.

Tips…Try to marinate the salmon for at least 30 minutes to get the maximum flavour. You could do it before you go to work, then cover and refrigerate until ready to cook.
…For an extra kick, try garnishing with half a finely diced red chilli.

Fiorentina crumpet pizza

Ⓥ **Serves 1 | 2½ *POINTS* values per recipe | Takes 10** minutes | **174** calories per serving

At the weekend, treat yourself to this delicious breakfast or brunch pizza.

> 1 crumpet
> low fat cooking spray
> 1 garlic clove, sliced
> 60 g (2 oz) baby leaf spinach
> 1 teaspoon white wine vinegar (optional)
> 1 egg
> 1 tablespoon tomato purée
> salt and freshly ground black pepper

1 Preheat the grill to medium and toast the crumpet for 2–3 minutes until golden on both sides.

2 Meanwhile, spray a non stick pan with the cooking spray, add the garlic and stir fry for 1 minute. Add the spinach and stir until just wilted. Season.

3 Bring a pan of water to the boil, add the white wine vinegar, if using (see Tip), and reduce the heat until just simmering. Break the egg into a small bowl and tip it into the water. Cook at simmering point for 2 minutes until the white is set then drain using a slotted spoon.

4 Spread the crumpet with the tomato purée. Top with the spinach and poached egg. Season and serve immediately.

Tip…White wine vinegar in the water can help your egg to set.

Ⓥ Variation…Use a plain white or wholemeal muffin instead of the crumpet for 3½ POINTS values per serving.

Quick classic pizza

Serves 2 | 12½ *POINTS* values per recipe | **Takes 20**
minutes | **315** calories per serving

One of the quickest pizzas ever.

> low fat cooking spray
> 23 cm (9 inch) ready made thin and
>   crispy pizza base
> **For the topping:**
> 65 g ready made tomato and garlic
>   pasta sauce
> 2 slices Parma ham, excess fat removed
>   and halved lengthwise
> 10 pitted black olives in brine, drained
> 50 g (1¾ oz) brown capped mushrooms,
>   sliced thinly
> 75 g (2¾ oz) light mozzarella, drained
>   and torn into pieces

1 Preheat the oven to Gas Mark 7/220°C/fan
oven 200°C. Spray a non stick baking tray with the
cooking spray and then put the pizza base on it.
Spread the base with the pasta sauce. Arrange
the ham slices around the base, then scatter over
the olives, mushroom slices and mozzarella.

2 Bake for 10–12 minutes until the pizza base is
browned and the cheese is bubbling. Cut in half
and serve immediately.

Spicy prawn open ravioli

Serves 2 | **10** *POINTS* values per recipe | **Takes 20** minutes |
202 calories per serving

> low fat cooking spray
> 4 spring onions, sliced
> 1 garlic clove, crushed
> 225 g (8 oz) tomatoes, chopped roughly
> 1 tablespoon fresh thyme leaves
> 4 tablespoons vegetable stock
> 1 teaspoon chilli flakes
> 1 tablespoon tomato purée
> 150 g (5½ oz) raw tiger prawns,
>   shelled (defrosted if frozen)
> 110 g (4 oz) frozen peas
> 165 g (5¾ oz) fresh lasagne sheets
>   (equivalent to 4 sheets)
> salt and freshly ground black pepper

1 Spray a large saucepan with the cooking spray
and heat until sizzling. Add the spring onions and
garlic. Cook over a medium heat for 3 minutes
until the spring onions have wilted. Add the
tomatoes and cook, stirring for 3 minutes until
the juices begin to run.

2 Add the thyme leaves, stock and chilli flakes
to the pan. Bring to the boil, reduce the heat
and simmer for 5 minutes until slightly thickened.
Season.

3 Stir in the tomato purée, prawns and peas and
cook for 3 minutes until the prawns have turned pink.

4 Bring a large pan of water to the boil, add the
lasagne sheets and cook for 2–3 minutes or according
to the packet instructions. Drain and rinse thoroughly.

5 Place a piece of pasta on each plate. Put a layer
of prawn and tomato mixture on top, add another
layer of pasta and then top with the prawn and
tomato mixture.

Italian Desserts

This chapter brings you traditional recipes that are low in **POINTS** values but still full of delicious and satisfying flavours. No matter which of these you choose to follow your pizza or pasta, you can afford to indulge in a **lovely Italian treat**.

Cassata

Ⓥ ❄ **Serves 6** | **21½ POINTS** values per recipe | **Takes 20** minutes + cooling + freezing | **244** calories per serving

3 tablespoons cornflour
600 ml (20 fl oz) semi skimmed milk
1 vanilla pod, split lengthways
½ x 405 g can skimmed, sweetened condensed milk
60 g (2 oz) mixed coloured glacé cherries, halved
25 g (1 oz) chopped glacé ginger
25 g (1 oz) chopped mixed peel
50 g (1¾ oz) raisins

1 Blend the cornflour with enough of the milk to make a paste and set aside. Place the remaining milk in a pan with the vanilla pod and bring slowly to the boil. Remove the vanilla pod, scrape the seeds from inside and stir them into the milk.

2 Stir the cornflour mixture. Add to the pan stirring continuously, then bring back to the boil. Simmer gently for 1–2 minutes until the sauce has thickened.

3 Add the remaining ingredients and stir to combine. Remove from the heat. Cover the surface with a piece of cling film. Set aside to cool completely.

4 Once the sauce is cool, pour into a freezerproof container, cover and freeze for 2 hours. Remove from the freezer and mash to break up any ice crystals, then return to the freezer for another 2 hours.

5 Repeat the mashing, then spoon the ice cream into a 450 g (1 lb) loaf tin, lined with cling film, and level the surface. Freeze until solid.

6 To serve, remove from the freezer 20 minutes in advance of serving and slice into six pieces.

Tip...To use an ice cream machine, once the sauce is cool in step 4, transfer it to the machine and churn according to the instructions. Serve immediately, as a soft scoop ice cream, or spoon into the loaf tin as in step 5.

Panettone

Serves 10 | **39 POINTS** values per recipe | **Takes 20** minutes to prepare + **50** minutes proving, **20–25** minutes to cook | **230** calories per serving

Here's a great alternative to traditional Christmas cake – it's much lighter and can be served for tea or toasted for breakfast.

350 g (12 oz) strong white flour, with
    2 teaspoons reserved for kneading
2 teaspoons dried instant yeast
50 g (1¾ oz) light brown sugar
1 teaspoon mixed spice
40 g (1½ oz) candied peel
finely grated zest of a lemon
finely grated zest of an orange
60 g (2 oz) sultanas
75 g (2¾ oz) low fat spread
25 g (1 oz) butter
100 ml (3½ fl oz) skimmed milk, plus
    1 tablespoon for glazing
2 egg yolks, beaten

1 Line the base and sides of a deep 20 cm (8 inch) cake tin with non stick baking parchment.

2 Mix together the flour, yeast, sugar, mixed spice, candied peel, lemon and orange zest and sultanas in a large bowl. Set aside.

3 In a small pan, gently melt the low fat spread and butter together. Add the milk and warm through for about a minute until hand hot. Make a well in the flour and add the milk and the egg yolks. Gradually draw the flour into the milk mixture using a wooden spoon. Mix to form a dough, using your fingers when the mixture gets stiffer.

4 Sprinkle the reserved flour on to a clean work surface and turn out the dough. Knead for at least 5 minutes until smooth and elastic. Return the dough to the bowl and cover with a clean tea towel. Leave in a warm, draught free place to prove for 30 minutes or until doubled in size.

5 Preheat the oven to Gas Mark 6/200°C/fan oven 180°C. Remove the dough from the bowl and knock it back, kneading it again for 3 minutes. Knead into a smooth ball, place in the prepared tin and stretch the dough out to the edges. Cover with a clean tea towel and leave in a draught free place to prove for 20 minutes or until doubled in size again.

6 Brush the top with 1 tablespoon of skimmed milk and bake for 20–25 minutes until golden. Cool for 5 minutes in the tin then remove to a wire rack to cool completely. Store in an airtight container for up to 5 days.

Tip...Traditionally, panettone is cylindrical, but you can bake it in a 900 g (2 lb) loaf tin if you prefer.

Crema Italiana

(2½ POINTS VALUE)

Serves 4 | **10½ POINTS** values per recipe | **Takes 25** minutes to prepare, **50** minutes to cook + chilling | **173** calories per serving

50 g (1¾ oz) caster sugar
For the coffee custard:
3 eggs
50 g (1¾ oz) caster sugar
225 ml (8 fl oz) skimmed milk
5 tablespoons freshly brewed strong espresso coffee
a kettleful of boiled water

1 Preheat the oven to Gas Mark 2/150°C/fan oven 130°C.

2 To make the caramel, put the sugar and 2 tablespoons of water in a saucepan. Heat over a low heat until all the sugar has dissolved, stirring occasionally and not allowing the mixture to boil, until all the sugar has dissolved. Once dissolved, turn up the heat and bring to a fast boil. Cook for about 10 minutes, swirling the pan occasionally, until the sugar is a dark golden colour – be brave and allow the caramel to darken without burning. Remove from the heat. Carefully and immediately, divide the mixture between four 150 ml (5 fl oz) ovenproof ramekins or mini pudding basins – a silicone spatula is useful for getting all the caramel out. Set aside.

3 Make the coffee custard. Beat the eggs and sugar together in a mixing bowl until well blended. Gradually add the milk and then the coffee, whisking well. Pour the mixture through a sieve into a jug, to remove the egg threads, then divide between the prepared ramekins.

4 Transfer the ramekins to a shallow roasting tray. Pour the boiling water into the roasting tray to come no more than halfway up the sides of the dishes. Carefully transfer the roasting tray to the middle shelf of the oven and bake for 50 minutes until set but still a little wobbly.

5 Carefully remove from the oven and allow the water to cool slightly. Remove the ramekins from the water bath and leave until cold then transfer to the refrigerator for at least 4 hours or preferably overnight.

6 To serve, run a sharp knife round the edge of each pudding, then turn out on to a serving plate, holding the two together. Shake sharply. You should hear the pudding release from the ramekin. Carefully remove to reveal the caramel sauce and serve immediately.

Italian desserts

Espresso biscotti

Ⓥ **Serves 8** (makes **16** biscuits) | **23 POINTS** values per recipe | **Takes 45** minutes to prepare + chilling + cooling, 25 minutes to cook | **193** calories per serving

> 225 g (8 oz) plain flour
> 75 g (2¾ oz) caster sugar
> 1 teaspoon ground cinnamon
> ½ teaspoon baking powder
> ½ teaspoon bicarbonate of soda
> 2 eggs
> 2 tablespoons espresso beans,
>   ground coarsely
> 1 teaspoon vanilla extract
> 25 g (1 oz) plain chocolate chips
> **For the topping:**
> 40 g (1½ oz) caster sugar
> ½ teaspoon ground cinnamon
> ½ teaspoon unsweetened cocoa powder

1 Mix the flour, sugar, cinnamon, baking powder, and baking soda together in a large bowl. Using an electric mixer on a low speed, beat the eggs into the flour mixture, one at a time, until well mixed, scraping down the bowl once or twice. Beat in the ground espresso beans and vanilla. If necessary, add water, 1 teaspoon at a time, to bring the dough together. Stir in the chocolate chips (the dough will be very thick). Turn the mixture out on to a clean work surface and knead briefly. Cover with cling film and chill until the dough is firm enough to be shaped (at least 30 minutes).

2 Preheat the oven to Gas Mark 4/180°C/fan oven 160°C. Line a baking tray with baking parchment. Stir together the topping ingredients and set aside.

3 Shape the chilled dough into two logs, about 2.5 cm (1 inch) wide, 20 cm (8 inches) long, and 1 cm (½ inch) thick. Sprinkle the topping mixture on to a clean work surface and carefully roll each log in the mixture until thickly coated. Transfer the logs to the prepared baking tray and dust generously with any remaining topping. Re-shape the logs if necessary, and flatten slightly so they are about 4–5 cm (1½–2 inches) wide.

4 Bake in the preheated oven until they are dry to the touch and a light golden brown around the edges, which should take about 20–25 minutes. Remove from the oven. Put the baking tray on a wire rack and leave to cool for at least 2 minutes.

5 Carefully remove each log from the baking tray and transfer to a cutting board. Slice the biscotti diagonally very thinly (about 1 cm/½ inch thick) into 8 biscuits each. If the biscotti crumbles when you do this, put it back in the oven for a few minutes to firm up a little more. Also, try to slice them with one swift motion so that the chocolate doesn't smear.

6 Lay the slices on the baking tray again, cut side down, and cook for a further 7 minutes. Remove from the oven and turn over. Cook for a further 7 minutes or until dry, and then transfer to a wire rack to cool completely. Store in an airtight container.

Zabaglione

Serves 2 | **7½ POINTS** values per recipe | **Takes 7** minutes | **464** calories per serving

This warm and foaming mousse is very rich so a little goes a long way. Zabaglione is quick to make but needs to be made at the last minute.

> 3 egg yolks
> 3 tablespoons golden caster sugar
> 3 tablespoons Marsala or sweet sherry

1 Place the egg yolks and sugar in a heatproof, medium size bowl over a pan of gently simmering water. Whisk together until they become thick and pale and have increased slightly in volume.
2 Add the Marsala or sherry and continue whisking until the mixture becomes warm and frothy.
3 Serve immediately in warmed glasses with the biscotti.

Tip… This is delicious with 1 Espresso Biscotti (see opposite, on page 60) for dipping, for an additional 1½ POINTS values.

Variation… Marsala is a fortified sweet wine and is available in most supermarkets and wine shops. Try this recipe with dark rum or whisky if you prefer and the POINTS values per serving will be 5½.

Pistachio ice cream

Serves 6 | **21½ POINTS** values per recipe | **Takes 20** minutes + freezing | **255** calories per serving

This delicately flavoured ice cream with pistachio nuts makes a great supper party treat.

> 4 egg yolks
> 6 tablespoons caster sugar
> 1 teaspoon cornflour
> 600 ml (20 fl oz) semi skimmed milk
> 110 g (4 oz) pistachio nuts, chopped finely
> 1 or 2 drops of green colouring (optional)

1 In a large bowl, whisk together the egg yolks, sugar and cornflour until pale and creamy.
2 Pour the milk into a medium sized pan, add the nuts and bring to the boil. Remove from the heat and whisk into the egg mixture slowly to avoid curdling. Return to the pan and cook over a low heat for 2–3 minutes until thickened; it should coat the back of the spoon. Stir in the green colouring, if using.
3 Pour into a freezerproof container and freeze for 2 hours or until semi solid. Remove from the freezer and mash, using a fork to break up large chunks of ice. Return to the freezer and freeze overnight.
4 Alternatively, use an ice cream machine to churn the mixture following the manufacturer's instructions, then serve immediately or freeze. To serve, remove from the freezer 20 minutes in advance. Serve two medium sized scoops per person.